Dear Mr. President

100 Earth-Saving Letters

Marc Davenport

A Citadel Press Book
Published by Carol Publishing Group

To Julie
who has made it possible for me to write.

A Citadel Press Book
Published by Carol Publishing Group
Citadel Press is a registered trademark of Carol Communications, Inc.

Editorial Offices: 600 Madison Avenue, New York, N.Y. 10022
Sales & Distribution Offices: 120 Enterprise Avenue, Secaucus, N.J. 07094
In Canada: Musson Book Company, a division of General Publishing Company
   Ltd., Don Mills, Ontario M3B 2T6

Queries regarding rights and permissions should be addressed to Carol
Publishing Group, 600 Madison Avenue, New York, N.Y. 10022

Carol Publishing Group books are available at special discounts for bulk
purchases, for sales promotions, fund raising, or educational purposes.
Special editions can be created to specifications. For details, contact:
Special Sales Department, Carol Publishing Group, 120 Enterprise Avenue,
Secaucus, N.J. 07094

 This book is printed on recycled paper. A portion of the author's royalties will
be donated to environmental organizations.

Manufactured in the United States of America

10 9 8 7 6 5 4 3 2 1

Library of Congress Cataloging-in-Publication Data

Davenport, Marc.
    Dear Mr. President : 100 earth-saving letters / Marc Davenport.
        p.   cm.
    "A Citadel Press book."
    ISBN 0-8065-1269-5 (pbk.) :
      1. Environmental protection—Forms.   2. Form letters.
    3. Environmental protection—United States—Directories.
    4. Environmental protection—United States—Information services—
    Directories.   I. Title.
    TD170.2.D38   1992
    363.7'0525—dc20
                                                    91–40813
                                                       CIP

Contents

Preface

Chances are you care what happens to the Earth and its inhabitants. You're probably concerned that our landfills are filling up and closing their gates. Maybe you want more recycling in your community. Doubtless you want to see an end to all the horrible environmental problems you have been hearing so much about—smog, acid rain, global warming, ozone depletion, deforestation, radioactive waste, groundwater pollution, species extinctions, and so on.

But how much impact can you have? Sure, you recycle your aluminum cans, but it's only the George Bushes and Lee Iacoccas of the world who have the power to really change things.

Don't sell yourself short.

While those people may do the actual weaving of society's tapestry, the threads come from you and me. Politicians do what they think their constituents want them to do because they want to be reelected. How do they know what their constituents want? By reading their letters. Business leaders try to provide goods and services consumers want because they want to make more money. How do they know what new products to offer? One way is by reading consumers' letters.

But who has time to sit down and write all those letters? How do you address a letter to the President? How do you find out who your federal and state legislators are, and what you say to them? How do you convince them? What facts do you cite? How do you persuade local store owners to stock recycled products? Where do you start?

Right here.

This book contains one hundred letters specifically designed to help save the environment. They are already composed, copyedited, and typed (on recycled paper). All you have to do is choose the letters you want, tear them out, address them (some are already addressed), sign them, and mail them. There are letters written to the President, members of Congress, local government officials, business owners and managers, friends, family members, and neighbors. But the letters needn't be sent to these particular people. Send them to anyone you wish. Or, if you don't agree with some of them, don't send them at all. Use them as springboards to write letters of your own.

Mark Twain observed, "Everyone talks about the weather, but no one does anything about it." Today you *can* do something about it—you can help reverse the greenhouse effect. And you can do lots of other things to save the environment—which is what everybody is talking about today.

Don't be a talker who does nothing. Make a difference. Buy yourself a copy of this book (if you haven't already bought one), sit down with a handful of envelopes, and start tearing pages out. If you have kids, let them help—they'll love the novelty of ripping pages out of a book and the excitement of mailing a letter to the President. They'll learn to respect and preserve the environment (if they're not already way ahead of you). They'll understand better how government and business work. And they might even learn how to compose and send a good letter, which could be one of the most important skills they ever learn.

Maybe you don't like this approach. That's fine. Do something else to save the environment. But please don't do nothing.

And don't wait too long; if we don't make some drastic changes soon, old Mother Earth is going to start treating us as carelessly as we have been treating her.

Acknowledgments

Many thanks to my wife, Julie, for her unwavering support and invaluable editing help, to Lee and Pat Killough, for their gracious advice and counsel, to my family and friends, who never lost faith in me, and to Rachel Carson, Jacques Cousteau, John Javna, Marjorie Lamb, Jon Naar, Carl Sagan, and all the others whose devoted efforts have made me and countless others see that we must all work together to save the Earth.

Introduction

Our environment is in crisis, and the situation is growing more urgent daily. You see the signs on TV and in the newspapers: half the world is choking on smog and drinking contaminated water; global warming may soon reach the point of no return; acid rain and radiation are killing forests, lakes, and crops; the Earth's rain forests and protective ozone layer may soon be gone; spilled oil, insecticides, herbicides, fungicides, rodenticides, fertilizers, and thousands of other chemicals are poisoning us; we are running out of places to dump our garbage; three species of life are becoming extinct every day...the list goes on and on.

As the Worldwatch Institute (a research organization based in Washington, DC) pointed out at the beginning of 1990, our present society is not sustainable. That is, it cannot satisfy our current needs without jeopardizing future generations. Worldwatch predicts that if we do not reverse our condition within the next four decades by recycling, conserving, replacing fossil fuels with alternatives, and measuring progress in terms of sustainability rather than growth, environmental and economic deterioration is likely to cause the disintegration of our society.

Other assessments are even more grave. Unless greenhouse warming is checked, it could eventually make the Earth too hot to live on. Unless ozone depletion is stopped, sunshine may become deadly to living things. Unless pollution and deforestation quit driving species to extinction, lack of biological diversity could cause our entire ecosystem to collapse.

What it all boils down to is this: Human beings are unwittingly destroying the planet. Unless we change the way we treat our environment, we may precipitate the extinction of civilization.

Clearly, each and every one of us is to blame. There is not a person on Earth whose actions do not have an impact on the environment. We Americans are particularly to blame since we consume more resources per capita than the people of any other nation. We all have an obligation to future generations to commit ourselves to saving the environment. And, if this planet with its marvelous diversity of life (including us) was created then we have an obligation to its creator to preserve it.

The most direct way you can help the environment is to stop ruining it yourself—by driving less, by boycotting harmful products, by recycling, and so on. If you don't already know what you can do to help, you will after reading a few of the letters in this book (be sure to look through appendix A, the environmental source list, in the back of the book too).

The next best way to help is to convince others that they should stop ruining the Earth too, and the surest way to do this is to write letters. Pick up any "save-the-environment" book, and you will read suggestions like "Write your representative" and "Let your grocer know you want additive-free food" and "If you don't like a company's product, make your opinion known" and so on. Letters are a powerful medium of persuasion, and we are fortunate to have the freedom of expression and the postal system that allow us to use letters to our advantage. Unfortunately, not enough of us have found the time to write the millions of letters that must be sent before industry executives, retailers, educators, lawmakers, government officials, and even our friends and neighbors can be persuaded to put environmental concerns at the tops of their lists. That is why this book was written.

A lot of people simply need to be educated.

Believe it or not, despite the media coverage ecological crises have received lately, many Americans have managed to remain ignorant of environmental problems. A few cogent facts in writing from a trusted friend, customer, or fellow worker may be all that is needed to shock them into awareness—and subsequent action.

Still more people know the Earth is in trouble, but they do nothing about it. Some of them procrastinate because they feel "too strapped for cash right now" to make any changes in their lifestyles, or because they don't realize how serious the problem is and think there is plenty of time to change later. Some would like to do something, but can't find time in their busy schedules to begin, or fear anything new, or are followers waiting for a leader, or are too stubborn to do anything until their neighbors do, or are simply so overwhelmed by the scope of the problem that they either don't know where to begin or think there is no chance of success. Some are just plain lazy. Many of these people may need nothing more than a little urging.

Some people refuse to acknowledge that our planet is in trouble. Others know they commit environmental mayhem, but have no intention of changing. These people are very hard to reach. Some of them either "don't give a damn," or believe some dogma like "God put nature here for us to subdue and use as we please." Most are simply slaves to their wallets and, although they sometimes bear burdens of guilt, cannot overcome their greed long enough to change.

Many of the people in this group can be persuaded, through the use of economic incentives, to make choices that help the Earth. For instance, if their customers quit buying their harmful products or services in favor of more benign ones offered by another supplier, they may begin offering better products. Sometimes the mere implication that customers are considering a boycott is all the impetus they need. And that implication can be voiced in a letter.

I have tried to keep each of these groups in mind while writing the letters in this book. For instance, when I wrote the letters in part II, I tried to craft them so they would appeal both to statesmen with integrity who care about the environment and to politicians who only care about being reelected. I hope each letter will educate some, urge others to stop procrastinating, and scare a few hard cases into doing the right thing even if they don't want to.

This book was written to be used, not to be read for entertainment as one reads a novel. I wouldn't recommend you read it straight through any more than I would suggest you curl up with a good dictionary. Although this book contains scores of different letters written for scores of different recipients ranging from your local grocer to the President, it includes a great deal of repetition of ideas and phrases because it is concerned with only a dozen interrelated themes. I do urge you to look through the entire book before deciding which letters to mail; you may find some you like better than others, and you may simply choose to use some as guides for writing letters of your own (which can be more specific and even more effective).

When you decide which letter to send first, read it carefully to make sure it says what you want it to say. Then tear it out of the book carefully, just as you would tear a check out of a checkbook. If you want to, trim the edge with scissors. If you have a typewriter, type the date, the name and address of the intended recipient, and your name and address, as shown in the sample letter (#0), and add any postscripts you think are needed; if you don't have a typewriter, print this information as legibly as you can. Then sign the letter before you send it.

You need not add your address to or sign any letters unless you are making copies of them (if you want to send the same letter to several recipients, be sure to read and understand the special copyright provisions in the front of this book before making copies). But I can assure you that a request bearing your name and address will be taken more seriously than an anonymous one.

This book does not claim to embrace every environmental issue or provide letters for all likely recipients. Instead, it tries to touch upon the major issues that affect everyone and provide a springboard, or starting point, for people who want to do something to help save the environment.

There are one hundred letters in all. Each is numbered in the upper-right-hand corner, opposite the date space (letters do not contain page numbers like the rest of the text). On the next page is a sample letter to show you where to add dates, names, and addresses.

Sample Letter

March 1, 1992   #0

John Q. Public
Acme Inc.
1000 Acme Drive
Anytown, N.Y. 00001

RE: A particular environmental issue

Dear Mr. (Ms.) Public:

This is to show you where and how to date, address, and sign the letters in
this book. If you are unsure of a person's gender, use the entire name
(Dear Terry Smith:). If you don't know the name, use Dear Sir or Madam:.

Sincerely,

Marc Davenport
c/o Citadel Press, Dept. MP
120 Enterprise Avenue
Secaucus, N.J. 07094

PART I

Letters to Businesses, Institutions, Organizations, and Individuals

Chapter 1

Letters to National and International Businesses

Junk Mail

The first letter in this book is already addressed to "Mail Preference Service." It simply asks that your name not be sold to mailing lists. What does that have to do with saving the Earth?

Plenty!

Every year, 100 million trees are sacrificed so that advertisers can stuff American mailboxes with junk mail we don't want. About 44 percent of it— enough to heat 110,000 homes every day—is never even opened. Instead, it is thrown in the trash, which means we pay an average of $65 per ton to have it hauled to our already overcrowded landfills, where it occupies valuable space for decades. Each American wastes an average of eight entire months of his or her life opening and reading the other 56 percent—and then throws almost all of that away too!

The paper industry is the largest single industrial user of fuel oil, and the paper bleaching process dumps deadly dioxins and furans into the environment. The inks that advertisers use often contain heavy metals and/or toxic solvents. And some of the plastics they use are not biodegradable (which means they occupy landfill space almost indefinitely) and produce toxic pollutants when they burn (which they often do, since landfills catch fire frequently).

All this wasteful activity causes deforestation, smog, acid rain, global warming, animal extinctions, and water pollution.

You and I and all the other consumers pay for junk mail because the companies that send it simply charge us more for their products to cover their advertising costs (or deduct the costs from their own taxes, which means we have to pay higher taxes to take up the slack). We pay for all the destruction it causes by paying higher health insurance premiums, by paying to clean up toxic waste, and by paying other expenses because "downstream" costs are not presently included in the prices of products. And we pay more to mail our letters than advertisers do for junk mail because they get bulk-rate discounts.

In other words, we are subsidizing junk mail and all the ecological havoc it causes, not just once, but several times!

By requesting that Mail Preference Service stop your name from being sold to mailing-list firms, you can prevent as much as 75 percent of the junk mail you would normally receive from ever being sent to you in the first place. You can stop even more of your junk mail by mailing a similar note to: Equifax Option, P.O. Box 740123, Atlanta, GA 30374–0123.

Socially Responsible Products

In some parts of the country, recycled paper products and other items designed to have a minimum impact on the environment are difficult or impossible to find. Residents of these areas who want to help save the planet must rely on mail-order

3

purchases from the small but growing number of companies that offer such products. Letter 2 thanks companies that sell "socially responsible" products, and asks for their catalogs.

Of course everyone's idea of what socially responsible means is different. There is no clear, objective line that can be drawn to separate all products into "good-for-the-environment" and "bad-for-the-environment" categories. Almost every product can be considered to have some negative effect, and every purchase involves compromises. For instance, you may find that toilet tissue made from recycled paper only comes wrapped in plastic, which many consider to be a no-no. But if you are concerned about saving the planet, you may decide to buy it anyway—after all, most regular supermarket toilet tissue comes wrapped in plastic too.

Several companies give you a chance to choose for yourself by offering a wide variety of products, many of which are generally considered to be much better for the planet than those you have become accustomed to seeing on your supermarket shelves. Earth Care Paper Company, for example, sells a full line of recycled paper products ranging from greeting cards to business envelopes, and donates 10 percent of its profits to environmental organizations. Seventh Generation also sells recycled paper products, as well as low-flow shower heads, cloth diapers, string bags, safe cleaners, etc., and donates 1 percent of its gross sales to a "Green Fund." Their addresses, and the addresses of other companies offering "environmentally superior" items, appear in appendix A.

A word of caution: Don't order an item just because it is sold by a particular company, or buy from a specific company just because it is mentioned in this book. Make your own informed, intelligent decisions about how you can best help the environment personally, and about which products you should buy.

Socially Irresponsible Products

Some products are so ecologically unsound that they can only be categorized as devastating to the environment, yet they continue to be sold in gigantic quantities, and more benign substitutes don't seem to have much of a chance to compete. The rest of the letters in this chapter are directed toward manufacturers and distributors of such products. The basic message each letter conveys is that you cannot in good conscience buy a particular product because it is harmful to the environment, but you *would* buy a substitute product that is not harmful. The idea is to wield a double-edged sword by appealing to whatever conscience company officials may possess while threatening the economic pressure of boycotting their product. This method can be very effective. Remember when Starkist Tuna changed its netting methods to stop killing dolphins in response to consumers' letters?

Letter 3 informs companies that make and distribute items containing ozone-destroying CFCs and halons that you cannot in good conscience buy their products until they begin substituting more benign alternatives. To find an address, look at the manufacturer's I.D. plate on a halon fire extinguisher, freezer, refrigerator, chiller, or automobile air-conditioner compressor. If no address is given, you may need to check an owner's manual or consult with a salesperson at the store where you bought the product. In some cases, it may be necessary to call a customer service representative or consult with a reference librarian to obtain the appropriate address. The CFCs contained in home air conditioners are not as damaging, but are nevertheless very harmful to the environment; home-air-conditioner manufacturers should not be overlooked as possible recipients of this letter. And if you know of a company that makes plastic foams, solvents, sterilants, or other products containing CFCs, you might want to send this letter there too.

Letter 4 asks magazine publishers to begin using recycled, recyclable paper instead of nonrecyclable, slick, coated paper. To find a publisher's name and address, simply leaf through the first few pages of an issue until you find the masthead page.

Letter 5 tells automobile manufacturers you are waiting until solar-powered, hydrogen-powered, or otherwise ecologically sound vehicles are available before buying again. At the time of this writing, the chairmen of the "big three" U.S. automakers are:

Lee Iacocca
Chairman of the Board
Chrysler Motors
P.O. Box 1919
Detroit, MI 48288

Harold A. Poling
Chairman of the Board
Ford Motor Company
The American Road
Dearborn, MI 48121

Robert Stempel
Chairman of the Board
General Motors Corporation
GM Building
3044 West Grand Blvd.
Detroit, MI 48202

Names and addresses of other executives can be obtained by calling a customer service number, which your local car dealer can give you. If you have only an address and no name, use the greeting: Dear Sir or Madam:.

Letter 6 tells a food company you are unhappy with its excessive, unrecycled, and/or unrecyclable packaging. A space is provided for you to name the product. Many processed foods display addresses on their labels. If yours does not, ask a store manager or visit your library. This is an area where consumer boycotts have been influential; witness the fact that processors have removed saturated fats, cholesterol, and sugar from some products because of economic pressure from consumers.

Letter 7 expresses your displeasure with the use of harmful phosphates in products like detergents. Again, a space is provided for the product name. As with processed foods, an address is often printed on the label.

Letter 8 concerns plastic dishes and utensils fast-food restaurants use in lieu of reusable or recyclable substitutes. To obtain an address, ask a restaurant manager.

Letter 9 is intended to pressure manufacturers of camp stoves to act more responsibly. If no address is printed on the product or its packaging, you can obtain one from a retailer who sells it.

_____, 199_

Mail Preference Service
Direct Marketing Association
11 West Forty-Second Street
P.O. Box 3861
New York, NY 10163—3861

Dear Sir or Madam:

Please do not allow my name to be sold to any mailing-list companies. I
will not open any unsolicited mail.

Thank you for your cooperation.

Sincerely,

—
—
—
—

_____, 199_

—
—
—
—

Dear Sir or Madam:

I understand your company is not only interested in the bottom line, but
cares about the environment as well. I want to thank you for having the
good sense to offer products that will allow us to take better care of the
planet we have so irreverently mistreated for so many years. Please send
me a copy of your catalog or other information on how I can begin
ordering ecologically sensible products. And keep up the good work!

Thank you for the material.

Sincerely,

—
—
—
—

—
—
—
—

RE: Chlorofluorocarbons and/or halons
_____

Dear Sir or Madam:

I understand your company sells products made with chlorofluorocarbons (CFCs) and/or halons, which are extremely harmful to the environment. I am writing to inform you that I cannot in good conscience buy your products until this practice is discontinued.

Scientists have determined that these chemicals are largely responsible for the destruction of the Earth's protective ozone layer. Studies show that as much as 6.2 percent of the ozone layer is already gone and that the rate of its deterioration is accelerating because the amount of these chemicals in the air is increasing. Each molecule of these chemicals can destroy up to ten thousand molecules of ozone in the upper atmosphere.

As more high-altitude ozone disappears, more ultraviolet solar radiation will leak through to the Earth's surface, damaging people and other living things. Popular accounts focus on the few thousand cases of skin cancer that are a likely short-term consequence, but the problem is much graver than that. We can also expect increases in cataracts and other signs of premature aging in humans and other animals; damage to immune systems; reductions in crop, timber, fish and ranch yields; upset of marine ecosystems; decreases in the size of plant foliage; and, eventually, a general decline, perhaps a total collapse, of the Earth's entire biosphere.

As if that were not enough, these same chemicals also cause up to 20 percent of greenhouse warming because they trap up to twenty thousand times as much solar heat as does an equal amount of carbon dioxide. And as greater volumes of them are released, that percentage—and the subsequent rate of global warming—will grow dramatically. So, even if efforts to replace fossil fuels with clean energy sources succeed, we will soon face rising seas and frequent, severe storms unless we stop releasing these substances.

Less harmful alternatives have been identified for nearly every application in which CFCs and halons are used. They are at present less convenient and/or initially more costly, but they are necessary—the price of not switching to them is unconscionable.

I urge you to begin using environmentally safe substitutes for CFCs and halons right away. By doing so, you will not only help save the environment, you will help yourself as well, since it is only a matter of time before all governments outlaw these chemicals.

Thank you for your consideration.

Sincerely,

___

___

___

___

—
—
—
—

RE: Recycled paper and nontoxic ink

Dear

Like many of your readers, I am concerned about environmental
deterioration. I am writing to inform you that although I like your
magazine, I cannot in good conscience continue to buy it until you begin
printing it on recycled, recyclable paper using harmless inks, as other
publishers have done.

Every year, 850 million trees are cut to make the 50 million tons of paper
Americans use. Much of the timber comes from the disappearing rain
forests that until recently have harbored half the world's animal and plant
species and have helped prevent a runaway greenhouse effect by absorbing
carbon dioxide and producing 40 percent of the oxygen in our atmosphere.
A large portion of the rest of the timber is cut from our own federal lands.
Most of the paper manufactured ends up in our landfills, exacerbating the
problem we face as we run out of room to dispose of solid wastes.

More than ten thousand U.S. landfills have been closed since 1979, and by
1995, twenty-four hundred of the six thousand now in operation will be
full. A substantial portion of landfill space is taken up by the 100 billion
pounds of wastepaper Americans discard each year. And a lot of that
wastepaper is in the form of magazines, which may take hundreds of years
to decompose, meanwhile emitting greenhouse gases like methane and
carbon dioxide, and leaching toxic compounds from their inks into the
groundwater that eventually becomes drinking water.

As if deforestation (and the subsequent extinction of species), global
warming, landfill overcrowding, and water pollution weren't damaging
enough, the paper industry also has the dubious distinction of being the
country's largest single industrial user of fuel oil, which means it
contributes greatly to smog and acid rain. And the industry's processes
use billions of gallons of our diminishing supplies of clean water and create
large amounts of deadly dioxins and furans.

Paper recycling can prevent a tremendous amount of environmental destruction. Every ton of recycled paper saves 17 trees, 7,000 gallons of water, and the equivalent of 4,100 kilowatt-hours of electricity or 380 gallons of oil—enough to heat the average home for six months—and keeps open as much landfill area as an "average" American uses in a year. Recycling also causes 35 percent less water pollution and up to 95 percent less air pollution than making paper from virgin fibers. Paper recycling creates jobs too—five times as many people are needed to produce a ton of recycled paper than are needed to put out the same amount of product using virgin wood pulp.

Unfortunately, no one has yet found a way to economically recycle slick magazine paper. So, with a few minor exceptions, every page of every issue of your magazine, instead of being a valuable resource that can be recycled, simply worsens the ecological crisis that faces us today.

According to the U.S. Environmental Protection Agency, 76 million of us are breathing dirty air. Some experts say as much as half of our drinking water is polluted. According to many ecologists, we are driving three species of life to extinction every day as we raze rain forests. Lakes, forests, and crops all over the northeastern U.S. and parts of Canada and Europe are dead or dying. And climatologists are predicting catastrophic rises in global temperatures due to the greenhouse effect. In other words, this planet is a sick patient.

We, and only we, are to blame for the Earth's sickness. And we, and only we, can bring about its healing. I am doing my part by boycotting products that make it worse and by sending letters like this one. I hope you will do your part by seeing to it that your publication starts using resources responsibly. If you do, please let me know so I can once again become a patron.

Thank you for your consideration.

Sincerely,

—
—
—
—

—
—
—
—

RE: Nonpolluting vehicles

Dear

Like many Americans, I am very concerned about environmental deterioration. I am writing to inform you that I will not buy a new car until nonpolluting vehicles are available.

Americans' cars produce twenty pounds of carbon dioxide for every gallon of gasoline they burn. That amounts to 4 billion pounds every day. And all of it gets pumped into the air, where it traps solar heat, causing a greenhouse effect. Climatologists and other scientists around the world say the concentration of atmospheric carbon dioxide is higher now than at any other time in history. Many believe this is why global average temperatures have risen measurably in the last century. They predict that if drastic measures are not undertaken soon to reduce carbon dioxide levels dramatically, global temperatures could rise by as much as nine degrees in the next few decades, melting the Earth's ice caps, flooding coastal areas, turning productive farmland into desert, and increasing the frequency and severity of storms.

Our cars also emit more than 8.5 million tons of nitrogen oxide (34 percent of the total) and more than 6.5 million tons of hydrocarbons (27 percent of the total) every year. These pollutants are responsible for a great deal of the smog that is choking people and vegetation, and the acid rain that is crumbling buildings and killing lakes, forests, and crops.

Government leaders have called for cars that get better gasoline mileage. Building them will ease the situation slightly, but not enough to avert disaster. At best it will amount to a myopic half-measure that ignores two important facts: Population growth and Third World development will still increase air pollution from vehicle emissions, and gasoline prices will continue to rise until the world's oil supply is depleted a few decades from now.

Alcohol and natural gas are already being used as vehicle fuel. They make more environmental sense than gasoline because they are inherently cleaner, but even they produce carbon dioxide and other pollutants. What are needed instead are production models based on prototypes that have performed well while producing little or no pollution—in other words, battery-powered, fuel-cell-powered, and hydrogen-burning vehicles, all of which can be recharged using pollution-free, 100 percent renewable solar energy.

I understand that your company cannot make as much short-term profit by building environmentally benign automobiles as it can by continuing to build gasoline-powered ones. But you and the other automakers need to understand that unless industries, including yours, start making environmentally sound decisions right away, you won't be able to enjoy your profits and you'll be out of business, because the planet is not going to be habitable. And even before that happens, government regulations, popular boycotts, rising gasoline prices, and oil depletion are going to shut down the manufacture of gasoline-powered cars anyway. As you know, California is already planning to phase them out.

I'm sure I'm not the first to present these facts to you and your company. I sincerely hope you take heed of them instead of pursuing the same self-serving path of short-term profits and long-term environmental catastrophe the American auto industry has steadfastly followed in the past. I hope you invest in the future by switching to renewable-energy-powered vehicles (and not fifty years from now or ten years from now, but today) instead of blindly clinging to the past, because the Earth is in terrible trouble, partly due to pollution from your products. And it's the only planet we can live on.

Thank you for your consideration.

Sincerely,

—
—
—
—

—
—
—
—

RE: Unacceptable packaging

Dear Sir or Madam:

I believe your company promotes environmental degradation by using too much packaging or packaging harmful to the environment. Until you change your packaging, I cannot in good conscience buy the following product(s):

The U.S. suffers from "packaging mania." In the past thirty years, the packaging we use has quadrupled. A tenth of all our grocery money—more than the net income of all our farmers—pays for it. Half the paper and plastic we discard—half the volume of all municipal wastes—is packaging. Three fourths of our glass, including 28 billion jars and bottles a year, is used for it. Packaging comprises 65 percent of all litter.

From an environmental point of view, the best kind of packaging is none at all, or as little as possible. When packaging must be used, reusable containers like glass soda bottles are best. Otherwise, the best materials to use are recycled and recyclable glass, aluminum, steel, and paper.

Unrecycled paper made from virgin wood fibers is a tragic environmental mistake. To make a ton of it, seventeen mature trees must be cut down. That means 425 million trees must die each year to make the paper packaging Americans discard. This is a loss we cannot afford, because trees not only provide us with food, wood, and shelter; they also stabilize soil and weather; shelter half the plant, animal, and insect species on Earth; provide half the oxygen we breathe; filter pollutants from the air; and prevent a catastrophic greenhouse effect by absorbing heat-trapping carbon dioxide.

We are rapidly deforesting the Earth; 87 percent of the ancient forest in the American Northwest has been harvested, and millions of acres of tropical rain forests are being razed yearly. Consequently, species are being driven to extinction faster than at any time in history, which could collapse our entire ecosystem. Scientists warn greenhouse warming could raise temperatures by as much as nine degrees in a few decades, flooding coasts, desiccating farmland, and intensifying storms. Clearly, we should not be killing trees for paper.

Recycling one ton of paper saves 17 trees, 7,000 gallons of water, and enough energy to heat an average home for six months. Recycling creates 35 percent less water pollution and slows smog, acid rain, and global warming by causing 74 percent less air pollution. Recycling also provides five times as many jobs as making paper from virgin fibers.

Most Americans prefer recycled, recyclable packaging, yet we continue using virgin-fiber packages and coating boxes with plastics and metal foils, which makes recycling impossible. Then these materials end up littering our highways, polluting our waterways, and being hauled to landfills and buried (at a cost to us of $65 per ton), where they occupy valuable space for decades or centuries.

Plastic packaging is equally undesirable. It is made from petroleum, a precious and dwindling nonrenewable resource, using processes that often generate toxic substances. Plastic packaging is not biodegradable, so it further aggravates landfill problems. Some types contain CFSs that destroy the Earth's protective ozone layer and exacerbate greenhouse warming. Some kill marine animals that become entangled in them or swallow them. Many types produce deadly gases when burned. And recycling of most plastics is not practicable.

A "disposable" society is not sustainable. If we continue it, we will use up all our resources. To make our system sustainable, we must forego a few short-term profits and stop the folly of things like individually-wrapped cheese slices and foil-lined boxes. If we keep making decisions that fail to protect the Earth, Homo sapiens may soon join the many species that have become extinct.

Thank you for your consideration.

Sincerely,

—
—
—
—

—

—

—

—

RE: Phosphates

Dear Sir or Madam:

I believe your company is promoting environmental degradation by using phosphates in its products. Until you change your formulas I cannot in good conscience buy the following product(s):

_____

Phosphates from dishwasher detergents and other products can kill lakes and streams by upsetting delicate ecological balances. As they leach into, or are dumped into, waterways, they can cause explosive growth of algae. When the algae die, bacteria that feed on them can use up so much of the oxygen in the water that other species like fish and plants cannot survive.

If all sewage passed through treatment plants that removed all phosphates and stored them in places where they could not reach waterways, detergents and cleansers containing phosphates would not pose such a serious problem. But sadly, a lot of sewage is dumped directly into waterways or into septic systems that leach into waterways, and many sewage-treatment facilities are not able to remove phosphates. And to complicate the problem, many streams and lakes are already overburdened by phosphates from agricultural and industrial chemicals they receive in runoff.

Since phosphates have been identified as being harmful to the environment, several companies have successfully developed alternative formulas for their products. I urge you to do the same. Please do your part to help save an environment that is already suffering from toxic dumping, deforestation, smog, acid rain, and greenhouse warming, and may be too ill to fight off yet another of humankind's thoughtless onslaughts.

Thank you for your consideration.

Sincerely,

—

—

—

—
—
—
—

RE: Harmful restaurant practices

Dear Sir or Madam:

I have observed that your restaurant uses disposable food containers and/or utensils that are not recycled. Because I believe this practice is harmful to the environment, I cannot feel comfortable about being a patron of yours until you change it.

The "disposable society" the U.S. has developed in recent years is a terrible environmental mistake. It depletes natural resources, overburdens landfills, encourages littering, and contributes to smog, acid rain, greenhouse warming, deforestation, water pollution, and the extinction of plant and animal species.

To make a ton of paper from virgin-wood pulp, seventeen mature trees must be cut down. That means 425 million trees must die each year to make the paper packaging Americans discard. This is a loss we cannot afford, because trees not only provide us with food, wood, and shelter, they also stabilize soil and weather, shelter half the plant, animal, and insect species on Earth, provide half the oxygen we breathe, filter pollutants from the air, and prevent a catastrophic greenhouse effect by absorbing heat-trapping carbon dioxide.

We are rapidly deforesting the Earth. Eighty-seven percent of the ancient forest in the American Northwest has been harvested, and millions of acres of tropical rain forests are being razed yearly. Consequently, species are being driven to extinction faster than at any time in history. This rapid change could collapse our entire ecosystem. Scientists warn that greenhouse warming could raise temperatures by as much as nine degrees in a few decades, flooding coasts, desiccating farmland, and increasing the frequency and severity of storms. Clearly, we should not be killing trees for paper.

Recycling a ton of paper saves 17,000 trees, 7,000 gallons of water, and enough energy to heat an average home for six months. Recycling creates 35 percent less water pollution than making paper from virgin wood fibers, and almost none of the deadly dioxins and furans that the original bleaching processes produce. It also helps prevent global warming and crop-destroying smog and acid rain by causing 74 percent less air pollution. And it provides five times as many jobs as making a ton of paper from virgin wood fibers. Yet, though most Americans care enough about the environment that they prefer recycled packaging, we insist on making food sacks and french-fry boxes out of virgin fibers. And we insist on coating cardboard boxes with plastics and metal foils, which makes recycling them impossible. All such materials end up littering highways, polluting waterways, or being hauled to landfills and buried (at an average cost to us of $65 per ton), where they occupy valuable space for decades or centuries.

Plastics are equally injurious. They are made from petroleum, a precious and dwindling nonrenewable resource, often using processes that generate toxic substances. They are not biodegradable, so they further aggravate landfill problems. Foam cups and plates release CFCs that destroy the Earth's protective ozone layer and exacerbate the greenhouse effect. They can injure or kill marine creatures that swallow them. They produce deadly gases when burned. And contrary to popular belief, they can only be made into things like picnic tables that are better made from other materials, not recycled into new cups and plates.

Our present "disposable" society is not sustainable. If we continue it, we will use up all our resources. To make our system sustainable, we must forego a few short-term profits and stop the folly of things like foam cups and plastic forks.

I urge you to switch to either reusable plates and utensils (which are best for the environment), or to recycled, recyclable paper plates (if you must use paper) and utensils made of materials that can be separated and recycled.

Thank you for your consideration.

Sincerely,

—
—
—
—

—
—
—
—

RE: Nonpolluting camp stoves

Dear Sir or Madam:

It is an unfortunate and curious fact that campers, who are among those most concerned about protecting wilderness areas, contribute to smog, acid rain, and greenhouse warming by producing hydrocarbons, nitrogen oxides, and carbon dioxide every time they use gasoline camp stoves.

I realize that camp stoves cause only a very tiny fraction of the air pollution that is destroying our environment. Utilities, refineries, other industries, and vehicles are principally to blame. However, it seems to me that since the stoves and the fuel come from the same suppliers and are sold side-by-side in the same retail outlets, and since so many of the customers who buy them are environmentally aware, camp stoves offer a splendid opportunity to demonstrate how clean, renewable energy alternatives can be substituted for ecologically harmful practices.

Hydrogen is the cleanest, most efficient combustible fuel there is. When it burns, it produces virtually no pollution—only a little pure water in the form of steam, and a lot of energy. It is so efficient, it is burned in the space shuttle's main engines. It can be made from water and solar or wind power using a simple process called electrolysis. And unlike gasoline, which will continue to rise in price until the world's petroleum supply is exhausted a few decades from now, solar energy, wind energy, and water are all 100 percent renewable.

Right now, hydrogen is a little more expensive than gasoline, but only because the downstream costs of gasoline (the costs of smog, acid rain, global warming, and environmental degradation due to leaking underground gasoline tanks, the medical costs of treating people with respiratory illnesses, etc.) are externalized. But in the near future, legislation being demanded by "green" movements around the world is bound to force internalization of these costs. And governments like the state of California are already making decisions that will phase out gasoline fuel entirely.

I urge you to jump on the "save-the-planet" bandwagon that is sweeping the world by designing and marketing hydrogen-fueled camp stoves and providing fuel for them in ecologically sound, reusable tanks. By doing so, you can make headlines, attract new customers by advertising your company as a leader in the environmental movement, discharge part of your responsibility to make amends for having sold environmentally harmful products in the past, help to preserve the nature that your customers go camping to enjoy, and be proud to share in redesigning our society so that we can live in harmony with nature instead of destroying it.

Thank you for your consideration.

Sincerely,

—
—
—
—

Chapter 2

Letters to Local Businesses and Institutions

The first six letters in this chapter appeal to the owners or managers of your local food markets. To obtain their names and addresses, simply ask the next time you shop there, or use your telephone directory.

Letter 10 asks that reusable shopping bags be provided.

Letter 11 asks a grocer to stock recycled products.

Letter 12 asks for phosphate-free products.

Letter 13 requests that more organic produce and additive-free products be sold.

Letter 14 is a plea for discontinuing the use of plastic foam trays.

Letter 15 asks that no beef from tropical countries where rain forests are being destroyed for pasture be sold. This letter could as easily be addressed to a butcher or a restaurateur as to a grocer.

In most cases, the next three letters can be sent to the same addresses you send your payments to. If you don't know the owner's or manager's name, call the number listed on your bill.

Letter 16 is written to owners or managers of garbage-collection companies. It asks them to provide or support curbside recycling.

Letter 17 asks your water utility to provide low-flow shower heads and other water-saving devices.

Letter 18 suggests that your electricity supplier replace its old facilities with new solar/hydrogen plants.

Letter 19 asks office-supply stores to stock and advertise recycled products.

Letter 20 asks members of your board of education to buy textbooks printed on recycled paper and to see that students are taught the importance of protecting the environment. Names and addresses are normally available by calling your local board of education, which should be listed in the telephone directory. If you can't locate the information you need, call a school in your district for help.

Letter 21 suggests to your child's teacher that he or she consider making an environmental issue the focus of a school project. This letter shouldn't need postage; your child can deliver it in person.

Letter 22 asks the owner of a day-care center (or anyone else who takes care of babies) to use cloth diapers instead of disposables.

Letter 23 is an appeal to hardware/lumber store owners or managers to stock nontoxic versions of such products as stains, lacquers, and cleaners.

Letter 24 is for automotive store owners or managers. It requests that they sell recycled motor oil and collect used oil to send on to recyclers.

The last letter in this chapter, letter 25, asks radio and television station owners or managers to devote a substantial portion of their public service announcement time to environmental topics.

Chances are good that you are personally acquainted with one or more of the businesspeople that these letters target, especially if you live in a small town or rural area. Because someone who knows you and respects your opinions is likely to think very seriously about what you have to say, your familiarity can be very persuasive.

On the other hand, telling a friend or professional contact something he or she does not want to hear may jeopardize your relationship with him or her. Be sure to take this into account before mailing any of these letters, particularly if you intend to have future business dealings with the intended recipients. If a letter is not couched in appropriate terms to convey the meaning you want to express to a particular person, try adding a postscript, or just use the letter as a guide and write a letter of your own. But don't inadvertently alienate important people in your community. Remember, you can do a lot more to save the planet if your credibility and influence are intact.

—
—
—
—

RE: Reusable shopping bags

Dear

While shopping at your store I noticed that you do not provide reusable shopping bags for your customers. This is of great concern to me, as I am trying to do all I can to help protect the environment.

As you may know, plastic bags are not biodegradable, which means they are filling up our landfills. Improperly disposed of, they can cause death or injury to animals and fish that become entangled in them or swallow them, and they have been known to suffocate children. They are made from crude oil, a nonrenewable resource that is rapidly being depleted, often using processes that create toxic pollutants. And the ink used to print advertising on them often contains toxic heavy metals that can contaminate our air and groundwater.

Paper bags can be recycled, but are often not made from recycled paper. Every seven hundred grocery bags represent the death of another mature tree. This is something we can ill afford, since our forests are being depleted at a frightful rate, and deforestation is one of the major causes of global warming.

Washable canvas or string bags are the best alternative. Some store owners have their store's name and location printed on them, and so receive free advertising as a bonus when customers take them to the beach or the laundry or carry books in them. You could charge five dollars for them and give buyers five dollars in store coupons to keep them coming back to your store. They are available from many sources throughout the country. Two sources for canvas tote bags are Save A Tree, P.O. Box 862, Berkeley, CA 94701, (510) 843-5233, and the Windstar Foundation, 2317 Snowmass Creek Road, Snowmass, CO 81654, (303) 927-4777. Two sources for string bags are Real Goods Trading Corporation, 966 Mazzoni St., Ukiah, CA 95482, (800) 762-7325, and Seventh Generation, Colchester, VT 05446-1672, (800) 456-1177.

The Earth is the only planet we have. Please help protect it by making reusable bags available to your customers.

Sincerely,

—
—
—
—

—
—
—
—

RE: Stocking recycled products

Dear

While shopping at your store, I saw few environmentally benign items—
cellulose sandwich bags, cloth diapers, paper towels made from recycled
paper, etc. I am writing to ask that you stock and prominently display
more items like these.

Deforestation has escalated to such a degree that unless significant changes
are made soon, all tropical rain forests and most other forests will be gone
within a couple of decades. Half the world's plant, animal, and insect
species could become extinct. Countless medicines and other forest
products will remain undiscovered. And the loss of biological diversity
could even collapse our own ecosystem.

Deforestation contributes to greenhouse warming, which may raise average
global temperatures by as much as nine degrees in the next few decades,
flooding coasts, desiccating farmland, and causing frequent, devastating
storms. It is conceivable that greenhouse warming could eventually make
the Earth too hot to support life.

Paper production is a major cause of both these problems. Because most
paper is made from virgin wood fiber, billions of trees are cut down to
make it. And the paper industry is our largest single industrial user of
fuel oil, which means it exacerbates global warming by releasing huge
quantities of carbon dioxide.

No trees need be cut to make tissues, napkins, and paper towels. Like
many other products, they can be made from recycled wastepaper. And
paper recycling helps prevent greenhouse warming because it uses 70
percent less energy. It also uses less water, cuts pollutants by half, and
creates five times as many jobs as making paper from virgin wood fiber.

Paper recycling also reduces landfill overcrowding. In the last eleven
years, ten thousand U.S. landfills have been closed, and twenty-four hundred
of the six thousand remaining are expected to close by 1995. Some cities

have instituted mandatory recycling because they cannot find space for new landfills. And nearly a third of our landfill space is occupied by paper, which may last for decades before disintegrating. Three cubic yards of landfill space is kept open every time a ton of paper is recycled.

Our fastest-growing landfill problem, though, is plastic. Most of it cannot be recycled economically. Because it is not biodegradable, plastic remains in landfills for hundreds of years (it already occupies a quarter of our landfill space). Plastic is made from petroleum—a precious, dwindling, nonrenewable natural resource—often using processes that cause toxic pollution. Many types of plastic release deadly gases when burned. And plastic waste is frequently dumped into waterways, where it often kills marine life that becomes entangled in it or swallows it. These are some of the reasons why we should be using natural, biodegradable cellulose fiber for food wrappers instead of plastic film.

Disposable diapers are an environmental nightmare. They contain both paper and plastic, and cannot be recycled. They account for a substantial portion of litter. They can also contaminate water supplies with dozens of diseases when they are discarded because landfills are not designed to handle the untreated sewage they contain. And more than a billion trees are cut each year to make them. Clearly, any store that sells them should at least also sell cloth diapers, which are cheaper, are biodegradable, and can be reused 100 times and then be recycled into industrial rags.

Unless we all help, attempts to save the environment may fail. Please do your part by stocking and prominently displaying the items I have mentioned. Two sources for them are Earth Care Paper Company, P.O. Box 7070, Madison, WI 53707, (608) 277–2900, and Seventh Generation, Colchester, VT 05546–1672, (800) 456-1177.

Thank you for your consideration.

Sincerely,

—
—
—
—

—
—
—
—

RE: Phosphate-free products

Dear

While shopping at your store, I was unable to find an ecologically safe,
phosphate-free dishwasher detergent. I am writing to ask you to begin
stocking and prominently displaying such products so that your customers
who are concerned about environmental degradation may buy them from
you rather than from another source.

Phosphates can kill lakes and streams by upsetting delicate ecological
balances. As they leach into or are dumped into waterways, they can cause
explosive growth of algae. When the algae die, bacteria that feed on them
can use up so much of the oxygen in the water that other species like fish
and plants cannot survive.

If all sewage passed through treatment plants that removed all phosphates
and stored them in places where they could not reach waterways,
detergents and cleansers containing phosphates would not pose such a
serious problem. But sadly, a lot of sewage is dumped directly into
waterways or into septic systems that leach into waterways, and many
sewage-treatment facilities are not able to remove phosphates. And to
complicate the problem, many streams and lakes are already overburdened
by phosphates from agricultural and industrial chemicals they receive in
runoff.

Since phosphates have been identified as being harmful to the
environment, several companies have successfully developed alternative
formulas for their products. One source for phosphate-free detergents is
Seventh Generation, Colchester, VT 05446—1672, (800) 456-1177; another is
Ecco Bella, 6 Provost Sq., Suite 602, Caldwell, NJ 07006, (201) 226-5799. I
urge you to contact these or other suppliers you may know of.

Please do your part to help save an environment that is already suffering from toxic dumping, deforestation, smog, acid rain, and greenhouse warming, and may be too ill to fight off yet another of humankind's thoughtless onslaughts. Please give your customers a chance to choose phosphate-free products.

Thank you for your consideration.

Sincerely,

—
—
—
—

—
—
—
—

RE: Organic and additive-free products

Dear

While shopping at your store, I found little organically grown produce and/or few additive-free food products. I am writing to ask you to stock and prominently display more such products so that your customers who are concerned about environmental degradation and about their health may buy them from you, rather than from another source.

Some fifty thousand varieties of pesticides are used on American food crops. Most have never been tested. Of those that have been tested, over one hundred ingredients used in them are suspected of causing cancer, birth defects, and/or gene mutations. And many of these ingredients will be absorbed into the food we eat and/or the water we drink. The EPA has already found seventy-four pesticides in the groundwater of thirty-eight states in the U.S.—the drinking water of half the American population.

Ironically, though they weaken the soil by attacking earthworms and microorganisms that normally keep it healthy, and though they sicken and kill birds, animals, fish, and people, these pesticides lack real effectiveness. Many pests have developed an immunity to them. Over 70 types of fungi and 440 types of mites and insects are resistant to pesticides. As a result, farmers lose about a third of their crops to pests, just as they did before pesticides were introduced.

Meanwhile, other chemicals exacerbate the situation. Artificial chemical fertilizers "rev up" plant growth to produce faster yields, but they also cause algae blooms that kill fish and other aquatic life in waterways, contaminate drinking water, and become absorbed into foods. Preservatives retard the growth of harmful bacteria, but they also retard beneficial bacteria, and they themselves may cause cancer. Mixed chemicals can result in a synergism, becoming more harmful in combination than they are individually.

Consequently, American food products are often not "good, wholesome food" at all, but a chemical soup containing herbicides, fungicides, insecticides, rodenticides, chemical fertilizers, preservatives, flavor enhancers, emulsifiers, and so on, any one of which may prove harmful to the people who consume them.

A 1988 Louis Harris poll found that 84 percent of American adults would rather buy organic foods that do not contain these contaminants. Were they to do so, they would improve the environment and the economy as well as their health. Aside from not eroding and wearing out soil and polluting water with pesticides and fertilizers, organic farms require less mechanization, which means less of the air pollution that causes smog, acid rain, and greenhouse warming. These farms also usually sell more of their products to local markets, so they require less transportation, which further reduces air pollution. And because weeds and bugs must be removed by hand, organic farms provide more jobs than equivalent mainstream farms.

In response to consumers' demands, grocers all over the country have begun offering more healthful, environmentally benign foods. I suspect a great many of your customers have already begun to shop at health-food stores or other markets to buy these products. As they continue to become more educated about health and about the environment, this trend is bound to escalate. I urge you to hold on to your customers and help save our beleaguered environment at the same time by stocking and advertising more organically grown and additive-free foods.

Supplier information is available from the Organic Foods Production Association of North America, P.O. Box 1078, Greenfield, MA 01301, (413) 774-7511.

Thank you for your consideration.

Sincerely,

—
—
—
—

—

—

—

—

<u>RE: Plastic-foam trays</u>

Dear

While shopping at your store, I was alarmed to see that fresh grocery items like meats are packaged in plastic-foam trays and wrapped in plastic. Because I believe this practice to be needlessly harmful to the environment, I cannot feel comfortable as one of your patrons until it is discontinued.

Plastics are made from petroleum, a precious and dwindling nonrenewable resource, often using processes that generate toxic substances. They can kill marine creatures that become entangled in them or swallow them. And they are not biodegradable, so they may take up valuable landfill space for hundreds of years (they already occupy a quarter of our landfill space, and are the fastest-growing form of refuse).

Plastic foams in particular can only be termed an environmental nightmare. Not only do they cause the problems mentioned above, but the chlorofluorocarbon (or CFC) blowing agents used to manufacture them also harm the Earth's biosphere by contributing greatly to both ozone depletion and greenhouse warming.

Studies show that as much as 6.2 percent of the Earth's protective ozone layer is already gone, and that the rate of deterioration is accelerating because CFCs are building up in the atmosphere. CFCs are largely responsible for the ozone depletion process because each CFC molecule can destroy up to ten thousand molecules of ozone.

As more high-altitude ozone disappears, more ultraviolet solar radiation will penetrate our atmosphere, damaging living things, including humans. Popular accounts have focused on the few thousand additional cases of skin cancer we are likely to see as a short-term consequence, but the problem is actually much worse than that. There will probably be increases in cataracts and other signs of premature aging in humans and other animals; damage to immune systems; reductions in crop, timber, fish, and ranch yields; upset of the fragile marine ecology; decrease in the size of plant foliage; and, eventually, a general decline, perhaps a total collapse, of the entire biosphere.

As if that were not enough, the same chemicals also contribute to the greenhouse effect because they trap up to twenty thousand times as much solar heat as does an equal amount of carbon dioxide. CFCs are already responsible for 15 percent to 20 percent of greenhouse warming. And as greater volumes of them are released, that percentage—and the subsequent rate of warming—will grow dramatically.

Scientists who are studying the greenhouse effect predict that unless drastic efforts to curb emissions of greenhouse gases are made very soon, average global temperatures can be expected to rise by as much as nine degrees in the next few decades. This climate change is projected to flood coastal areas, turn farmland into desert, and increase the frequency and severity of storms. But while most studies only speculate about the next few decades, greenhouse warming is progressive, and might eventually heat the Earth's atmosphere to such an extent that no life could exist here.

Clearly, we must abandon "use-it-once-and-throw-it-away" disposable plastic foams if we are to save our planet from environmental catastrophe. But, although many governments have already agreed that CFCs should be phased out eventually, and foam packaging has already been banned in Vermont; Maine; Berkeley, California; and Suffolk County, New York, we may not be able to stop the manufacture of these materials in time to save ourselves unless we all act now.

I am doing my part by boycotting plastic foams whenever possible, and by writing letters like this one. Please do your part by taking plastic foams out of your store.

Thank you for your consideration.

Sincerely,

—
—
—
—

—
—
—
—

RE: Rain-forest beef

Dear

Some beef comes from tropical countries where rain forests are being destroyed to graze cattle. Since I am very concerned about the health of the environment, I am appalled at this ecologically devastating practice, and cannot in good conscience buy any beef raised in this manner. I strongly urge you to take steps to prevent any such beef from ever entering your establishment, to buy American beef instead, and to let your customers know you are doing so.

Tropical rain forests are vital to our environment. They harbor over half of all plant, animal, and insect species, and are the source of 40 percent of the oxygen that living things, including humans, must have to survive. They filter pollutants out of the air—including the carbon dioxide that is the major cause of global warming. They prevent erosion and flooding, stabilize rainfall, and provide people with shade, evaporative cooling, food, wood, paper, medicines, and more.

Nevertheless, these rain forests are being razed at the rate of five acres per minute. That's an area the size of Ohio every year. By the year 2000, 80 percent of them may be gone. Already, about three species of wildlife are becoming extinct every day. Entire ecosystems are threatened with collapse, and plants that may have contained cures for cancer and AIDS will never be examined.

Some of this destruction is due to logging, but a large part of it results when cattle ranchers use slash-and-burn methods to carve vast areas out of the forests to make more grassland for their herds. Ironically, grazing turns such ranches into eroding deserts in only a few years because rain-forest soils are poor and thin, and because the trees must be present to prevent erosion.

If this process is not stopped, global warming and the extinction of species could escalate to catastrophic proportions. Rising sea levels, changing regional temperatures, and an increase in the frequency and severity of storms could bankrupt our economy and the economy of the world. And we might find that without the diversity of species that preserves the health of ecosystems, we may be incapable of sustaining our own food chain because of insect swarms or other unforeseeable conditions.

I urge you to join those of us who are determined to help save the planet by stopping deforestation. Please buy only American beef, and make a public declaration today that you will not buy any "rain-forest beef."

Thank you for your consideration.

Sincerely,

—
—
—
—

_____, 199_

—
—
—
—

RE: Curbside recycling

Dear

My purpose in writing is to urge you to establish or support curbside recycling in our community.

Some ten thousand landfills in the U.S. have closed since 1979, and twenty-four hundred of the six thousand that remain may follow by 1995. We are filling up old ones faster than we can find places for new ones because we are so wasteful. We generate more waste than any other nation—enough to fill a 145,000-mile convoy of garbage trucks every year. This year we will discard enough glass bottles and jars to fill the World Trade Center's two skyscrapers twenty-six times, and enough plastic bottles to fill four hundred miles of dump trucks. We will throw out 100 billion pounds of wastepaper, as much iron and steel as our automobile industry uses, enough aluminum to rebuild all our commercial airplanes four times, 300 billion pounds of compostable grass clippings, leaves, etc., and forty-one times as much motor oil as was spilled by the Exxon Valdez.

All of these discarded commodities are potentially valuable resources. Compost, for instance, is highly valued as a substitute for expensive chemical fertilizers. And in 1990, Americans earned nearly a billion dollars recycling aluminum cans. But amazingly, only a tenth of our waste gets recycled, whereas Japan reclaims 51 percent, some European cities recover as much as 65 percent, and, during a ten-week test program, one hundred East Hampton, New York, families recovered 84 percent.

Recycling can save enormous amounts of natural resources and keep tremendous quantities of carbon dioxide, nitrogen oxide, hydrocarbons, dioxins, and other pollutants out of the environment. Recycling "tin" cans saves 74 percent of the energy needed to make them from scratch and causes 76 percent less water pollution and 85 percent less air pollution. Recycling a ton of aluminum cans saves 177 million Btus of energy and thousands of pounds of raw materials, and keeps 789 pounds of solid waste and 76 pounds of air pollutants out of the environment. Recycling a ton of wastepaper can save 19 million Btus of energy, 7,000 gallons of water, 17 trees, 3 cubic yards of landfill space, and keep up to 60 pounds of pollutants out of the air and water (recycling also creates more jobs than making paper from virgin pulp).

Yet, instead of recycling, most Americans pay an average of $65 per ton in transportation and disposal fees to bury our trash in landfills, where it may last for hundreds of years. What this means is that we indirectly subsidize smog, acid rain, global warming, deforestation, the extinction of species, and the pollution of our drinking water, while at the same time running out of space for landfills and unnecessarily accelerating the depletion of our natural resources. This makes about as much sense as burning money and inhaling the smoke! What we should be doing instead is recycling as much as possible and profiting, both economically and environmentally, from the savings.

Over six hundred American communities have already begun to use curbside recycling because it is the most effective method of waste management available. The city of Seattle's program of charging customers by the pound for unseparated trash has been particularly successful. Rockford, Illinois, pays out disposal-cost savings to residents in a "trash lottery." And in the first two years of its beverage-container recycling program, New York State saved over $119 million in waste disposal, cleanup, and energy costs, and created thirty-eight hundred new jobs.

Clearly, the future of waste management is with curbside recycling. As environmental deterioration and depletion of resources continue, it will be adopted in more and more communities around the world. Eventually it will be adopted here. When that happens, I hope you will be one of those who can proudly say, "I was responsible!"

Thank you for your consideration.

Sincerely,

—
—
—
—

—
—
—
—

RE: Low-flow shower heads, etc.

Dear

The purpose of this letter is to urge you to consider supplying water-saving low-flow shower heads, faucet aerators, and toilet dams to your customers.

Clean water is fast becoming scarce in the U.S. We are using up our supplies faster than they are being replaced.

About half the U.S. population relies on groundwater, much of which is "fossil water" from ancient geologic formations that took hundreds of thousands of years to fill. Increases in population and irrigation are causing this water to be depleted so quickly that some large groundwater supplies are expected to play out within fifty years. Already many wells are running dry.

The other half of our population uses surface water, which is also in short supply in some regions. In parts of the West, rivers have been completely dewatered, their entire flows diverted to supply cities. Court battles over water rights—between individuals and even between state governments—are common. In Florida, so much water has been diverted for human use that the Everglades are drying up. In recent years, many U.S. communities have had to ration surface water because of successive years of drought. Now climatologists are predicting that these droughts may not be freak occurrences at all, but rather may represent a change in the Earth's climate brought about by greenhouse warming. They suggest that droughts may continue to grow worse for decades.

Both surface water and groundwater are becoming more contaminated all the time. A study conducted by the Environmental Protection Agency identified seventy-four pesticides in the groundwater of thirty-eight states. This is not surprising, since most of the 12 million tons of pesticides we spray on our forests, lawns, lakes, and food crops every year eventually washes into lakes and streams or seeps into the ground. It is, however, very unfortunate, since groundwater that has been contaminated may stay contaminated for decades. In Massachusetts, nine municipal wells and one hundred private wells recently had to be closed because they were tainted with road salt, a common pollutant in northern states. Almost every area of the country suffers from contamination of water supplies by industrial waste and municipal sewage that are dumped directly into streams; by gasoline from an estimated 500,000 leaking underground gasoline storage tanks; by the 365 million gallons of motor oil Americans pour into their toilets and driveways each year; and/or by a host of other pollutants such as acid rain, herbicides, landfill leachates, animal waste, and radioactivity from nuclear plants.

The bottom line is that there is not enough clean water to go around, and both water treatment and sewage treatment are constantly becoming more difficult and more expensive. Clearly, we must all try our best to avert disaster, not only by stopping pollution, but by conserving water as well.

Three simple, relatively inexpensive plumbing improvements—low-flow pulsating or aerated shower heads, toilet dams, and faucet aerators—can allow an average household of four people to save thirty-two thousand gallons of water per year without even noticing the difference. By buying large quantities of these devices, utilities can provide them to customers very economically. In many cases, the resultant decrease in water demand will obviate the need for investing in new treatment, pumping, and storage facilities, thereby offsetting the cost of the devices.

Two sources that distribute all three of these items are Ecological Water Products, Inc., 266 Main St., Suite 18, Medfield, MA 02052, (508) 359-5001, and Real Goods Trading Corporation, 966 Mazzoni St., Ukiah, CA 95482, (800) 762-7325.

Thank you for your consideration.

Sincerely,

—
—
—
—

—
—
—
—

RE: Solar power plants

Dear

The purpose of this letter is to urge the abandonment of any plans for new nuclear or fossil-fuel-fired generating plants in favor of plants based on some form of solar energy.

Nuclear accidents cannot be prevented, even when billions are spent on "fail-safe" backup systems. Nuclear Regulatory Commission documents show that more than thirty-three thousand accidents occurred in U.S. power plants since the 1979 incident at Three Mile Island. A thousand of these are considered significant. Testifying before the U.S. House of Representatives' Energy and Power Subcommittee in 1986, NRC Commissioner James Asseltine suggested a serious accident is likely in the U.S. within two decades. The probability of a major core-melt during that period has been put at 45 percent by an NRC projection.

Such an accident would be catastrophic. The Chernobyl debacle in 1986 displaced 135,000 people from 179 villages; killed 31 people; irradiated so many that tens of thousands of cancer deaths, birth defects, and genetic mutations are expected; contaminated huge amounts of crops, livestock, and wildlife in several countries; and cost the Soviets $13 billion (including the loss of the power plant). An Atomic Energy Commission study done years ago estimated that a meltdown in the U.S. could injure 73,000 and kill 27,000, while causing $17 billion in property damage.

So-called "inherently safe" reactors may be feasible to build decades from now, but even they are untenable because of the spent fuel they will generate. Such waste already presents serious problems. It stays radioactive for fifty thousand years and cannot be safely disposed of. Voters don't want it near them, so they defeat dump-site proposals, and the waste is temporarily stored. By the year 2001, we may have seventy-two thousand tons of this type of nuclear waste (as well as enough milling and mining waste to build a ten-foot-high-wall from coast to coast).

Fossil-fuel-fired plants are little better. Their smokestack emissions cause acid rain which poisons drinking water, crumbles buildings, and has killed lakes, crops, and forests in the U.S., Canada, and Europe. They are also a major cause of greenhouse warming, which may raise global average temperatures by as much as nine degrees during the next few decades, flooding coasts, desiccating farmland, spawning frequent, terrible storms, and conceivably making the Earth too hot to live on. These emissions are also one of the reasons 76 million Americans are breathing dirty air. Furthermore, fossil fuels are valuable, nonrenewable resources that will continue to rise in price until they are depleted during the next century.

Clean, renewable photovoltaic, solar-thermal, wind, small hydroelectric, ocean-thermal, and tide energies are free, inexhaustible, 100 percent renewable, and available domestically in huge amounts. Each is virtually pollution-free. And when used in conjunction with water electrolyzers, each of these energies can be converted into hydrogen, which forms almost no pollutants at all when burned, and which can store off-peak power and fuel everything from power plants to furnaces to automobiles.

All the technology needed to convert to renewable energy and hydrogen storage is already being used by industry. Electricity from most renewable sources, although cheaper than nuclear power, is a bit more costly now than electricity from coal-fired plants. However, if downstream costs of burning coal are included in the equation (medical costs of treating people who breathe dirty air; losses of crops, fish, and buildings to acid rain; the expense of protecting coastal areas from ocean levels that will rise because of the greenhouse effect; etc.), renewables are already cheaper. And since governments are sure to force internalization of these costs soon, solar energy is a wise choice economically as well as ecologically.

Thank you for your consideration.

Sincerely,

—
—
—
—

—
—
—
—

RE: Recycled office supplies

Dear

The purpose of this letter is to urge you to help save the environment by stocking and advertising recycled computer paper, copier paper, ruled pads, stationery, and other paper products.

American office workers discard an average of over 175 pounds of high-grade paper per person every year. The copier, computer, and typing paper we threw away last year would have been enough to build a wall nearly one and a half feet tall all the way around the world.

Most of that waste paper could have been recycled through a process that uses 50 percent less water, 74 percent less energy, and 100 percent fewer trees than making paper from virgin wood fiber (about seventeen mature trees are ground into pulp to produce a ton of new paper), while at the same time producing 74 percent less air pollution and 35 percent less water pollution, and creating five times as many jobs. But we didn't recycle much of it. Instead, we spent an average of $65 per ton to bury it in landfills, where every ton of it occupies about three cubic yards of space.

We did this despite the fact that paper, which can last for decades when buried, is filling our landfills up so quickly that municipal authorities around the country are racking their brains to find enough space to build the five hundred new ones that are needed each year. We did it even though cutting trees for pulp is a major cause of the deforestation that kills three species of life per day, and helps cause the global warming that could flood coasts, desiccate farmland, and spawn terrible storms within the next few decades. And we did it in spite of the fact that virgin-pulp production pollutes streams with deadly dioxins and furans and contributes to the acid rain that poisons water supplies, crumbles buildings, and kills lakes, forests, and crops.

Recycled paper has a hard time competing. Virgin-pulp paper is usually cheaper because the downstream costs of making it (costs of medical care for people who breathe dirty air, crop and timber losses and building damage due to acid rain, protection of coasts from flooding due to greenhouse warming, etc.) are externalized, and because the government indirectly subsidizes the timber industry. But more paper would be recycled if more recycled paper products were sold. And more such products would be sold if more buyers were offered a choice and an explanation of why that choice is important. Some consumers would understand that everyone ultimately pays hidden downstream costs anyway (through higher insurance premiums, higher taxes, and price hikes), so recycled products aren't really more expensive. And others would choose recycled paper, regardless of the cost, just to help the environment.

Everyone pays for his or her choices. We have made a lot of harmful choices in the past, and because of them the only planet we can live on is in trouble—which means you and I are in trouble.

Now we have a chance to make some smart choices. I believe I made one when I decided to send this letter. I hope you will make one too. I hope you will invite everyone to come to you for recycled office supplies. And I hope you will tell them why you are doing so.

Thank you for your consideration.

Sincerely,

—
—
—
—

—
—
—
—

RE: Environmentally friendly textbooks

Dear

Children learn by example, and we adults are the only examples they have. If children are to care about the environment, I believe it is crucial for them to see that we care. If we expect them to make ecologically sound choices in the future, they must see us making them now.

But educators all over this country habitually make one particular choice that is extremely injurious to the environment, and they do it literally right under the noses of every young student they try to teach. On every school day of every year, almost every student in America holds in his or her hands a textbook printed on paper that was not recycled.

Many of the 850 million trees that are pulped each year to make the 50 million tons of paper Americans use are cut from the disappearing rain forests that until recently have harbored half the world's land species and have helped prevent a runaway greenhouse effect by absorbing carbon dioxide and producing 40 percent of the oxygen in our atmosphere. Many others are cut from our own national forests. Either way, cutting them causes deforestation and contributes to erosion, global warming, and the extinction of biological species.

The paper industry itself contributes greatly to smog, acid rain, and global warming because it is the largest single industrial user of fuel oil. And its processes use billions of gallons of our diminishing supplies of clean water and create large amounts of deadly dioxin.

Recycling is much better for the environment. Every ton of recycled waste paper saves 17 trees, 7,000 gallons of water, and the equivalent of 4,100 kilowatt-hours of electricity or 380 gallons of oil—enough to heat the average home for six months. It also causes 35 percent less water pollution and up to 95 percent less air pollution, and keeps open as much landfill area as an average American uses in a year. And recycling creates jobs—five times as many people are needed to produce a ton of recycled paper than are needed to put out the same amount of paper made from virgin wood pulp.

The Earth is in terrible trouble. We are filling her atmosphere with hydrocarbons, oxides of carbon, nitrogen, and sulphur, and a host of other harmful gases. We are dumping pesticides, sewage, and toxic industrial wastes into her waters. We are gouging out her minerals, stripping her of her forests, and driving her wondrous species to extinction by the thousands.

The consequences of our actions are clear. Clean water is growing scarce. Smog is choking us to death and killing vegetation. Acid rain is decimating fisheries, forests, and crops, poisoning water supplies, and crumbling buildings. Oceans are dying, and cities are drowning in their own refuse. The atmosphere is getting hotter; within a few decades greenhouse warming may flood coastal areas, turn farmland into desert, and increase the frequency and severity of storms. And every year, all living things are in more danger from the sun's deadly ultraviolet radiation because the Earth's protective ozone layer is disappearing.

Regardless of our present efforts to wrestle with these problems, our kids are going to inherit them. They will grow up with them, they will suffer because of them, and they will have to try to solve them.

I urge you to help our children and our environment at the same time. Please ensure that students are taught reasons and techniques for protecting the Earth, and then reinforce their instruction, first by buying textbooks printed on recycled, recyclable paper, and then by telling the children why.

Thank you for your consideration.

Sincerely,

—
—
—
—

_____, 199_   #21

—
—
—
—

RE: Environmental school projects

Dear

As an ecology-minded parent, I hope every parent conveys the importance
of protecting the environment to each of his or her children, but I fear we
are not doing enough in this regard. As the world's population continues
to increase, it appears we are rushing headlong toward environmental
catastrophe. And it is our children who will inherit our legacy of smog,
acid rain, global warming, deforestation, ozone depletion, water pollution,
extinction of species, and wasteful use of resources. It is our children who
will have to know how to deal with these problems long after we are gone.

Teaching children statistics about the dismal threats our ecosystems face
today probably serves little purpose other than to frighten or depress
them. But hands-on projects that imbue them with a sense of how fragile
and marvelous and important our environment is, and that give them a
chance to interact with it directly, may fire them with enthusiasm to save
it.

I hope you will investigate environmental subjects like conservation,
recycling, composting, organic gardening, etc., whenever you have
opportunities to offer special projects to my child's class and future classes.

Two good sources for ideas are the Earth Works Group's 50 Simple Things
Kids Can Do to Save the Earth (Kansas City, MO: Andrews and McMeel,
1990), and Marjorie Lamb's 2 Minutes a Day for a Greener Planet (San
Francisco, CA: Harper & Row, 1990). If you want to see something other
students have accomplished, contact Creating Our Future, 1640 Francisco
St., Berkeley, CA 94703, (510) 841–3020, and ask about How to Organize a
Rainforest Awareness Week at Your School, an information packet made up
by high school students.

Thank you for your consideration.

Sincerely,

—
—
—

_
_
_
_

RE: Disposable diapers

Dear

I understand that you use disposable diapers. These products are
extremely injurious to the environment. The purpose of this letter is to
urge you to substitute ecologically safe cloth diapers whenever possible.

Every year, a billion trees are cut and turned into pulp to make disposable
diapers. This is something the Earth cannot afford, because it is rapidly
being deforested. In tropical rain forests, an area the size of Washington
state is cleared every year, and all of the United States' intact old-growth
forests may be gone by 1995.

Deforestation is driving thousands of plant and animal species to
extinction, including those that might have provided cures for cancer or
AIDS. It also fuels the greenhouse effect because trees remove most of the
heat-trapping carbon dioxide from the air. Scientists predict that if
deforestation is not moderated, greenhouse warming could cause coastal
flooding, turn farmland into desert, and increase the severity and
frequency of storms within the next few decades.

The processes used to make disposable diapers from raw materials use up
tremendous amounts of energy and produce pollution that contributes to
the acid rain that is poisoning our water supplies and killing forests,
fisheries, and crops.

Even throwing disposable diapers away causes problems. Every year,
Americans discard 18 billion of them—enough to circle the Earth 120
times. Some disposable diapers contribute to the growing collection of
litter along our streets and highways. Others end up in waterways, where
they poison the water and kill marine creatures that try to eat them. Most
are buried in landfills at a cost of 4 percent to 20 percent of the cost of the
diapers. They now account for up to 4 percent of the space in our
landfills. But landfills are filling up so quickly that we are running out of
places to put the five hundred new ones that are needed each year, and

disposable diapers, which contain plastic, can last five hundred years. And since people often don't dispose of the waste they contain before throwing them away, they carry an estimated three million tons of untreated human waste and one hundred viruses into landfills, which are not designed to accept sewage, and which may allow it to leach into water supplies where it becomes a serious health hazard.

No trees are cut to make cloth diapers, and they decompose in a few months in landfills. They are also cheaper in the long run; they can be reused up to one hundred times (and then recycled into industrial rags). Even those provided by diaper services often save users 25 percent to 35 percent. Cloth diapers are also better for babies. Disposables hold in all moisture, which can raise skin temperature by as much as four degrees, and can cause severe rashes. In studies, babies wearing them suffered rashes five times more frequently than those wearing cloth diapers.

Most disposable diapers are bought for convenience. But because diaper services are now available in many areas, and because cloth diapers now come prefolded and diaper pants with Velcro fasteners are available, cloth diapers are no less convenient. I urge you to at least try using them for a while. Try them, and then pat yourself on the back for doing something to help save the environment.

To find out where your nearest diaper services are located, you can write to the National Association of Diaper Services, 2017 Walnut St., Philadelphia, PA 19103, or call (215) 569–3650. If you are interested in special natural-fiber diaper products, contact Baby Bunz and Company, P.O. Box 1717, Sebastopol, CA 95473 (707) 829–5347, or Bio-Bottoms, P.O. Box 6009, 617C Second St., Petaluma, CA 94953, (707) 778-7945.

Thank you for your consideration.

Sincerely,

—
—
—
—

—
—
—
—

RE: Environmentally friendly products

Dear

The purpose of this letter is to ask you to stock and advertise products like nontoxic stains, lacquers, and cleaners, as well as biodegradable herbicides and pesticides.

The Earth is in terrible trouble. We are filling her atmosphere with hydrocarbons, oxides of carbon, nitrogen, and sulphur, and a host of other harmful gases. We are dumping pesticides, sewage, and toxic wastes into her waters. We are gouging out her minerals, stripping her of her forests, and driving her species to extinction by the thousands.

The consequences of our actions are clear. Millions have suffered illness or death from cancer and birth defects. Clean water is growing scarce. Smog is choking us to death and killing vegetation. Acid rain is decimating fisheries, forests, and crops; poisoning water supplies; and crumbling buildings. Oceans are dying, and cities are drowning in their own refuse. The atmosphere is getting hotter; within a few decades greenhouse warming may flood coastal areas, turn farmland into desert, and increase the frequency and severity of storms. And every year, all living things are in more danger from the sun's deadly ultraviolet radiation because the Earth's protective ozone layer is disappearing.

If we are to survive as a species, each and every one of us must do what he or she can to stop the polluting of this planet. After all, it is the only planet we have, the only place we can live.

Nearly every hardware center in the country is contributing to the ruination of our environment by selling a wide variety of toxic materials. Many paints, stains, and lacquers contain lead, cadmium, toluene, benzene, or other highly toxic components. These can cause illness to those who inhale them and pollute water supplies when people pour them into drains or bury them in landfills. Some cleaners also contain highly toxic chemicals and they are almost always poured into sewers. Pesticides and herbicides, which are routinely poured or sprayed directly on lawns, fields, and gardens, where they wash into or leach into water supplies (and are frequently applied directly to fruits and vegetables), are often highly poisonous and nonbiodegradable. Charcoal-starter fluid contributes to greenhouse warming, and probably to acid rain and smog as well. The chlorofluorocarbons in refrigerant gases and plastic-foam insulations are the major cause of ozone depletion. Phosphates contained in detergents and chemical fertilizers can kill waterways by promoting "algae blooms." And so on.

I strongly believe that hardware store owners and managers and others who sell such products have a responsibility to offer environmentally benign alternatives, and I think they should make customers aware of exactly how using these alternatives can help prevent damage to the environment.

One source for ecologically benign alternatives is Seventh Generation, Colchester, VT 05446–1672, (800) 456–1177. Another is Sinan, P.O. Box 857, Davis, CA 95617–0857, (916) 753–3104. I urge you to investigate these suppliers or others like them you may already know about.

Thank you for your consideration.

Sincerely,

—
—
—
—

—
—
—
—

RE: Recycling motor oil

Dear

The purpose of this letter is to urge you to help the environment by
stocking and advertising the sale of recycled motor oil and by accepting
recyclable used crankcase oil from your customers.

Used crankcase oil has become a serious environmental problem. Motor
oil is toxic to most forms of life to begin with, and used oil generally
contains additional poisons like bearing metal. One quart of motor oil can
contaminate 250,000 gallons of drinking water or form an oil slick over
almost two acres of a lake or pond. So it is essential to dispose of it
properly.

Unfortunately, a tremendous amount of the motor oil used in the U.S. is not
disposed of safely. Last year, approximately 365 million gallons of it were
poured into sewers or on driveways, or dumped in other places where it
could eventually find its way into water supplies. That's forty-one times as
much oil as was spilled by the Exxon Valdez in Prince William Sound,
Alaska. An estimated 2.1 billion tons of oil ended up in waterways,
accounting for about 40 percent of water pollution.

Used motor oil can be re-refined. It takes less than two quarts of it to
produce a quart of new oil, whereas forty-three quarts of virgin crude oil
would be required to make the same amount. Every quart that gets re-
refined saves eleven thousand Btus of energy because re-refining requires
only one third as much energy as refining from petroleum. But most
people don't recycle their used oil because they can't find a convenient
place to take it. And most people don't buy re-refined oil because they
don't know it exists or because they don't find it on the shelves of the
stores where they buy their automotive supplies.

Please help to protect our mistreated environment and our rapidly
dwindling supply of clean drinking water by collecting used motor oil and
passing it along to recyclers, and by stocking re-refined oil on your shelves
and making sure your customers know about it.

One source for re-refined motor oil is Seventh Generation, Colchester, VT 05446–1672, (800) 456–1177. To find out who picks up used oil in this area and to obtain a copy of the Used Oil Recycling Newsletter, contact the Environmental Protection Agency, 401 M St., SW, Washington, DC 20460–0001, (202) 260–7751.

Thank you for your consideration.

Sincerely,

—
—
—
—

—
—
—
—

RE: Environmental public-service announcements

Dear

As I understand it, your station broadcasts a certain number of public service announcements, the content of which are at least partially left to the station's discretion. I am writing to ask that as much of your air time as possible be devoted to environmental issues.

Charities and scouting and the like are very important, but I believe that if we are to survive as a species, all other issues must occasionally take a backseat to efforts to save the Earth from destruction by human actions.

Our planet is in terrible trouble because of us. We are filling her atmosphere with hydrocarbons, oxides of carbon, nitrogen, and sulphur, and a host of other harmful gases. We are dumping pesticides, sewage, and toxic industrial wastes into her waters. We are gouging out her minerals, stripping her of her forests, and driving her species to extinction by the thousands.

The consequences of our actions are clear. Clean water is growing scarce. Smog is choking us to death and killing vegetation. Acid rain is decimating fisheries, forests, and crops; poisoning water supplies; and crumbling buildings. Oceans are dying, and cities are drowning in their own refuse. The atmosphere is getting hotter; within a few decades greenhouse warming may flood coastal areas, turn farmland into desert, and increase the frequency and severity of storms. And every year, all living things are in more danger from the sun's deadly ultraviolet radiation because the Earth's protective ozone layer is disappearing.

The warnings of scientists are growing more urgent each day. In order to avert catastrophe, perhaps the end of all life on this planet, we must stop deforestation and begin reforesting the Earth; we must conserve our natural resources through reduction, reuse, recycling, and more efficient designs; we must develop clean, renewable energy alternatives; we must prevent nuclear accidents and the use of nuclear weapons; and we must stop polluting our air and land and water.

Each thirty-second on-air promotion of a hazardous-waste collection project, recycling drive, or environmental awareness effort has a great potential to lead to substantial improvement of the environment by making people aware of what problems are facing us and of how they can help to solve them. Please give as much consideration as you possibly can to each request for a PSA involving the environment.

Thank you for your consideration.

Sincerely,

—
—
—
—

Chapter 3

Letters to Friends, Relatives, and Organizations

You should already have the addresses you need for the letters in this chapter. They were written for members of your family, friends, neighbors, fellow workers, and members of organizations like your scouting group, fraternity, or sorority.

The first two are personal letters. Closings have purposely been omitted so that you can add a personal note and your own special closing.

Letter 26 tells a friend about this book.

Letter 27 suggests using recycled gift wrap, greeting cards, etc., to have an "environmental holiday season" this year.

Letter 28 suggests a neighborhood meeting on the environment.

Letter 29 suggests to a group (scouts, baseball team, drama club, etc.) that it consider selling recycled paper products instead of candy or cookies during fund-raising drives.

Letter 30 was written to be posted on a bulletin board at your workplace to help in organizing car pools.

Letter 31 suggests to a fraternity or other organization you belong to, or are acquainted with, that it choose an environmental issue for one or more of its future community projects.

Dear

I have found a book that I want to recommend to you. It's <u>Dear Mr.</u>
<u>President: 100 Earth-Saving Letters</u>, written by Marc Davenport and
published by Citadel Press in 1991.

This book is a collection of full-sized (8½″ × 11″) letters, all printed on
recycled paper. They're written so you can send them to the President,
members of Congress, mayors, business leaders, teachers, store owners—all
kinds of people who can help the environment in one way or another. You
just tear the pages out, sign them, copy them if you want, address them, and
mail them. As a matter of fact, this very letter is one of the pages.

<u>Dear Mr. President</u> gives you addresses for people like the chairmen of the
boards of directors of the big automakers, the EPA, your governor, your U.S.
senators and representative. Imagine how fast your representative will
come up with a clean water bill or an antinuclear bill or a bill to stop acid
rain if half the people in his district send him one of these letters telling
him they want one. The book also includes addresses and phone numbers
for all sorts of environmental organizations, like the Sierra Club and the
World Wildlife Fund, and for companies that sell everything from recycled
gift wrap to cloth diapers to solar power plants.

The book doesn't tell you something vague like "write your
representative" or "let your board of education know how you feel" or "tell
the manufacturers you don't like the way their products are packaged."
Instead, it gives you clear, concise letters that are ready to be mailed. Each
letter cites relevant facts and figures and spells out exactly what people
need to do. There are letters about smog, acid rain, greenhouse warming,
deforestation, radioactive pollution, toxic dumping, recycling, energy
alternatives, and other environmental issues. You don't have to spend half
a day figuring out how to address them and the other half deciding what to
write. And knowing that a lot of other people are going to send the same
letters to the same people gives you a good feeling. It makes you feel like
something positive will happen.

<u>Dear Mr. President</u> should be available at any bookstore. If a store
doesn't have it, they should be able to order it for you. Or you can order it
directly from Carol Publishing Group by sending a check or money order
for $12.95 plus $3.00 for shipping and handling to 120 Enterprise Ave.,
Secaucus, NJ 07094, or by calling (800) 447-BOOK(2665) and using your
Visa or MasterCard.

Dear

 I have been thinking a lot about the environment lately. It seems like every place you look you see something about deforestation, or acid rain, or the greenhouse effect, or the extinction of species, or about the importance of recycling cans and planting trees. So I am thinking about having an "environmental holiday season" this year—and maybe every year.

 People are doing lots of things during the holidays that can help save the Earth. Some are buying recycled gift wrap and greeting cards. Some are buying live Christmas trees and planting them after Christmas. Some are giving gifts like memberships to the Cousteau Society, solar battery chargers, and books about how to help save the environment. Others are avoiding rain-forest beef and being careful not to buy things made out of teak or redwood, so as to help reduce deforestation and greenhouse warming. Still others are turning their thermostats down for a few days or making a special effort to reuse and recycle things.

 I am going to do a few things to include the Earth in my holiday plans this year. Would you like to join me? I am sure if we put our heads together, we can come up with some great gift ideas for the environment.

—
—
—
—

Dear

I have been thinking a lot about the environment lately. It seems like
every place you look you see something about deforestation, or acid rain, or
the greenhouse effect, or the extinction of species, or about the importance
of recycling cans and planting trees. I think we should have an
"environmental block party" to determine what we can do here in our
neighborhood to help save the Earth.

My idea is to invite people in our immediate neighborhood to meet and
discuss things like recycling and planting trees, to see if there are things
we could cooperate on to help the environment. Neighborhoods in some
cities have done things like setting up car pools, voting on one trash
collection company for the whole neighborhood, or giving the whole
neighborhood's raked leaves to someone who needs fill instead of sending
them to landfills. Surely there must be something we can feel good about
doing here.

I would appreciate your input on the subject. Specifically, I would like to
know:

1. Where should an environmental issues meeting or party be held?

2. Would you be able to host such an event?

3. When should it be held/not be held?

4. What issues should we plan to discuss?

Thank you for your help. I can be reached at:

Sincerely,

—
—
—
—

—
—
—
—

RE: Selling recycled products to raise funds

Dear

I wonder if you have thought of selling recycled products for future fund-raising projects?

From my point of view, too many fund-raising projects involve sales of cookies or candy, or focus on walk-a-thons or jog-a-thons. Everybody likes cookies, but they really aren't very good for us, and a lot of people either can't eat them or choose not to. Walk-a-thons can be fun, but they waste a tremendous amount of physical effort that could be used to accomplish some very important work.

By selling recycled products, organizations not only make money and teach responsibility, they also provide residents with items like recycled toilet tissue, which everyone can use and which may not be available to them otherwise. And most important, they do something to help the environment, which is now in such a state of crisis that everyone really should be doing something to save it.

Making almost any product from recycled materials helps the environment. For instance, recycling paper reduces deforestation, greenhouse warming, smog, acid rain, water pollution, and the extinction of plant and animal species. For every ton of paper recycled, seventeen mature trees, seven thousand gallons of water, and enough energy to heat the average home for six months are saved, and as much landfill area as an average American uses in a year is kept open. And making paper from wastepaper provides five times as many people with jobs as making it from virgin wood pulp.

Several companies sell recycled products. One company in particular, the Earth Care Paper Company, even has a special fund-raising program. All the necessities are provided, including fund-raising brochures, order forms, product samples, and complete instructions. A curriculum source list and educator's study guide are also included so schools can offer "an educational recycling curriculum unit." And Earth Care even awards prizes to participants who sell the most. More information can be obtained by writing to Earth Care Paper Company, P.O. Box 7070, Madison, WI 53707, or by calling (608) 277–2900.

Many companies that supply recycled products nationwide either have programs of their own set up, or would be happy to work with you on yours. Most environmental organizations can recommend suppliers. Or, if you want a complete listing of products containing recycled materials and their manufacturers and distributors, contact American Recycling Market, P.O. Box 577, Ogdensburg, NY 13669, (800) 267–0707, and ask how to obtain their Recycled Products Guide.

Thank you for your consideration.

Sincerely,

—
—
—
—

—
—
—
—

OPEN LETTER

TO: Anyone who drives to work regularly

RE: Carpooling

Dear

The Environmental Protection Agency says that the air in areas where more than 76 million Americans live doesn't meet clean-air standards. One reason is because the air is full of automobile exhaust. Auto emissions account for 27 percent of the hydrocarbons that form smog, which ruins people's lungs and kills vegetation, and 34 percent of the nitrogen oxide that contributes to acid rain, which pollutes water supplies, crumbles buildings, and kills fisheries, forests, and crops.

Cars also give off carbon dioxide, which is the chief cause of greenhouse warming. For every gallon of gasoline a car burns, it emits about twenty pounds of carbon dioxide—nationwide, that adds up to about 2 million tons every day. Scientists predict that greenhouse warming could raise average global temperatures by as much as nine degrees over the next few decades, causing coastal flooding, turning farmland into desert, and increasing the frequency and severity of storms.

Carpooling provides an opportunity to combat these problems and at the same time reduces our dependence on foreign oil, saves on gasoline costs, and avoids "driver stress." About a third of all "car-miles" are driven to and from work, with each commuter car carrying an average of only 1.3 people. Were each car to transport three riders instead, ten thousand tons of carbon dioxide would be kept out of the air and a million gallons of gasoline would be saved every day. And drivers who live just eight miles from work could avoid twenty-five hundred miles of nerve-racking driving each year by sharing their driving equally.

I urge everyone who drives to work to save money, reduce your stress, and help an environment that is in terrible trouble. Please, talk to others—find out if you can join an existing car pool or form a new one.

Thank you for your consideration.

Sincerely,

—
—
—
—

—
—
—
—

RE: Environmental projects for organizations

Dear

I am writing to ask that your organization consider choosing activities
that will in some way help the environment for your future community
service projects.

The Earth is in terrible trouble. We are filling her atmosphere with
hydrocarbons, oxides of carbon, nitrogen, and sulphur, and a host of other
harmful gases. We are dumping pesticides, sewage, and toxic industrial
wastes into her waters. We are gouging out her minerals, stripping her of
her forests, and driving her species to extinction by the thousands.

The consequences of our actions are clear. Clean water is growing scarce.
Smog is choking us to death and killing vegetation. Acid rain is
decimating fisheries, forests, and crops, poisoning water supplies, and
crumbling buildings. Oceans are dying, and cities are drowning in their
own refuse. The atmosphere is getting hotter; within a few decades
greenhouse warming may flood coastal areas, turn farmland into desert,
and increase the frequency and severity of storms. And every year, all
living things are in more danger from the sun's deadly ultraviolet radiation
because the Earth's protective ozone layer is disappearing.

These problems did not occur spontaneously. They are the results of
human negligence. And if they are to be solved, everyone must pitch in
and help. In light of these facts, I believe all service organizations should
consider environmental projects when planning for the future. Possible
activities might include tree plantings, trash pickups, wildlife research,
recycling and precycling campaigns, composting projects, establishment
and maintenance of wilderness areas, monitoring of pollution, education
projects, and scholarships for students working to better the environment.
Additional ideas can easily be obtained by contacting any environmental
organization.

Please join the growing number of concerned people trying to be part of the solution rather than part of the problem by posing a challenge to the other members of your organization. The next time they are deciding how best to help make their community a better place in which to live, please ask them if they would first consider working to make the Earth a place where human beings can continue to survive.

Sincerely,

—
—
—
—

Chapter 4

Letters to the Editor

This chapter makes use of an extremely important medium of communication in a democratic society: the letter to the editor.

Almost any of the letters in this book could have been designed to be sent to newspaper publishers as candidates for publication in their op-ed sections, but I have limited the letters in this chapter to subjects that seem to have had little editorial exposure in the past, that are so universal that it would be difficult to target any one recipient, that might offend your friends and neighbors were you to broach them personally, or, as in the case of letter 34, that deal with a subject that applies to newspaper publishers themselves.

If any of the other subjects examined in this book have not been given enough attention by local newspapers, I suggest your write some of your own letters to the editor in addition to the ones in this chapter. You can usually find the address you need by reading the page on which letters to the editor appear—often the page opposite the editorials.

The first letter in this group, letter 32, explains how the methods we use to build and maintain our lawns may damage the environment.

Letter 33 explains how the charcoal in barbecue grills can be started without using ecologically damaging charcoal lighter.

Letter 34 challenges publishers to print their newspapers on recycled newsprint.

Finally, letter 35 suggests people buy recycled greeting cards, recycled wrapping paper, Christmas trees that can be planted, etc., in order to have an "environmental holiday season."

—
—
—
—

RE: Lawns and the environment

Dear Editor:

When most people look at a pretty green lawn they don't see the damage it may be doing to the environment. I think we need to step back for a moment, look at our lawns from a different perspective, and ask ourselves if they are really what we want.

Ecosystems have evolved slowly over eons. Living things develop through natural selection and adaptation, and are affected by complex relationships with the Earth, weather patterns, and millions of other species. Almost any change in the environment, however slight, can have far-reaching ecological consequences, a few of which we can predict and many of which we cannot even begin to imagine. Some can be catastrophic. Yet we are currently engaged in systematic global efforts to destroy and replace the marvelous diversity of what might be termed "God's handiwork" with lawns.

The typical human attempt at "land improvement" begins by scraping every tree and living thing off the land with bulldozers or whatever other means are available. This can destroy even the beneficial microorganisms in the soil. Animals and insects flee, upsetting the balance of other areas, and many die. Instead of being relocated or composted to produce new soil, uprooted plants are normally burned—not in power plants where they could produce electrical power, but in the open air, where they contribute to air pollution.

Once this slaughter is complete and we have sealed a portion of the land over with concrete or asphalt (ensuring that nothing can grow on it for decades or centuries), we set about replacing the hundreds of species that once inhabited the remaining area with a single species of grass, or at most three or four species. These grasses are seldom prepared to survive; they are chosen for appearance, not because they are native to the area. In many cases, they are not even natural species; instead they have been developed through our manipulation of genes.

We could help our lawns survive by letting them grow. This would let them reseed themselves. It would also allow strong roots to form and prevent soil drying, lessening the need for watering. Instead, we keep them in a permanent state of injury by cutting them with mowers that help deplete another natural resource (petroleum). Cutting weakens our lawns to such an extent that we must use huge quantities of our dwindling water supply to keep them alive. Even so, they may die unless we use up even more resources to make poisonous chemicals to pour on them so that better-adapted species will not eat them or crowd them out. And finally, instead of letting the mulch from our mowers act as a natural fertilizer to renew the poisoned soil, we put it in nonbiodegradable plastic bags and pay an average of $65 per ton to send it to overcrowded landfills, and then spend more money and use up still more resources for powerful chemical fertilizers.

Lawns often absorb hundreds of times less greenhouse-effect-causing carbon dioxide from the air than the original trees, shrubs, and weeds. Herbicides, insecticides, and fungicides we spray on them can eventually find their way into drinking water supplies and perhaps cause cancer or birth defects. Fertilizers wash away into waterways to cause unnaturally large algae blooms that can smother other aquatic life. Deforestation changes natural weather patterns. Pollutants from chemical plants, refineries, and mowers contribute to water pollution, smog, acid rain, and greenhouse warming. Much of the water we use to keep our lawns alive comes from geologic and glacial formations which took millions of years to form, and which will eventually be depleted. And watering over long periods salinizes soil, ruining it.

Let's plant more trees. Let's let our grass grow a little taller, and then leave the cuttings where they fall. And let's think twice before we clear land or spray poisons on the ground.

Sincerely,

—
—
—
—

—
—
—
—

RE: Charcoal lighter and the environment

Dear Editor:

Most of us love to cook outdoors, or to eat food that has been cooked outdoors. There probably isn't a town in America where the mouth-watering aroma of food cooking over charcoal fires can't be detected on summer evenings. But charcoal grills, like so many other things, can have a harmful impact on the environment, and if we want to continue using them we should use them responsibly.

It is the charcoal-starting fluid that causes problems. It is a fire hazard. It contributes to smog, acid rain, and greenhouse warming. It may leave toxic residues in food. And empty lighter fluid containers, which users must dispose of, are technically hazardous waste because they still contain a small amount of flammable liquid.

Some would argue that singling out charcoal-lighter fluid seems ridiculous in light of the tremendous amounts of toxic waste, power-plant exhaust, sewage, and other pollutants that are dumped into our environment on a regular basis. But the truth is that all sources of pollution must be reduced. And lighter fluid is such a substantial contributor to smog that the city of Los Angeles, California, has banned its use, effective January 1992.

Fortunately, lighter fluid is not an essential ingredient of the charcoal broiler. Electric heating elements designed to ignite charcoal briquettes are available at many supermarkets and hardware stores. Charcoal chimneys are probably the best alternatives from an environmental standpoint. Anyone can make one by punching air holes in the bottom and around the bottom circumference of a large coffee can with an old-fashioned "church key" can opener.

To use a charcoal chimney, place it on the grate in the bottom of your grill so that air can circulate up through it and put wadded newspaper in the bottom of it. Then add charcoal and light the bottom of the newspaper through one of the air holes. After fifteen minutes, you can remove the chimney with a pair of pliers or tongs and spread the charcoal.

Manufactured charcoal chimneys complete with handles are available from environmental product supply houses and at some department and hardware stores. One source for them is Seventh Generation, Colchester, VT 05446-1672, (800) 456-1177.

As the environment becomes more and more polluted, legislation may eventually force everyone to give up things like charcoal-lighter fluid. We may even have to give up gasoline-powered cars. But I believe that instead of waiting for politicians or circumstances to dictate to us what we must do, each of us should decide what we should do. I hope most people will decide, as I have, to do more to save our environment. This is, after all, the only planet we have to live on.

Sincerely,

—
—
—
—

—
—
—
—

RE: Printing newspapers on recycled paper

Dear Editor:

More than 850 million mature trees are ground into pulp to make the 50 million tons of paper used every year in the United States. Because of the methods used to harvest pulp trees and the fact that trees cannot be replaced at nearly the rate they are being destroyed, the pulp industry is a major cause of deforestation, which in turn contributes to soil erosion, desertification, greenhouse warming, and the extinction of plant and animal species. The pulping and bleaching process uses tremendous amounts of our dwindling clean water supplies, pollutes streams with deadly dioxins and furans, and generates solid waste. And the paper industry is the largest single industrial user of fuel oil, which means it generates substantial quantities of the air pollutants that ultimately contribute to smog, acid rain, and global warming.

Newspapers are part of the problem. More than 62 million of them are printed every day in this country. That kills a lot of trees—more than 26 million every year just for our Sunday papers (it takes 75,000 trees to make a Sunday edition of the New York Times). Most of the newsprint our papers are printed on comes from Canada, which now cuts 247,000 more acres trees than it replants every year.

About seventeen mature trees are required to make a single ton of newsprint from virgin wood pulp. The process also uses about 28 million Btus of energy, 24,000 gallons of water, 360 pounds of salt cake, 216 pounds of lime, and 76 pounds of soda ash, and generates 176 pounds of solid waste and 120 pounds of air and water pollutants.

Once the newspapers are printed, we read most of them once and pay an average of $65 per ton to bury them in landfills, where every ton of them takes up three cubic yards of space for years or decades (archaeological studies of landfills have found that some newspapers are still legible after having been buried for twenty years). Unfortunately, the nation's landfills are filling up faster than we can find places to build the five hundred new ones that are needed each year. Some ten thousand have closed since 1979, and twenty-four hundred of the six thousand that are now being used will be full within five years.

We need not deplete our resources and wreak havoc on the environment; newsprint can be made from recycled wastepaper. Recycling consumes no trees and up to 60 percent less water and 70 percent less energy; causes 35 percent less water pollution and up to 95 percent less air pollution; and creates five times as many jobs as virgin-pulp processing. The bleaching process generates dioxin when paper is made from virgin pulp; recycling, which requires less bleaching, creates less dioxin. And if just half the newsprint in the U.S. were recycled, we could keep thirty-two hundred truckloads of wastepaper out of our landfills every day.

Recycled newsprint is not as expensive or as scarce as some people claim. Some suppliers even buy waste newspaper from communities whose newspaper publishers contract to buy newsprint from them, which can result in partial subsidies from local governments desperate to reduce the amount of solid waste they must landfill. One such company, FSC Paper Corporation, supplies paper made of 100 percent recycled fiber to the Chicago Sun-Times, which has been using 30 percent or more recycled newsprint successfully for about twenty years.

Because of the tremendous environmental damage the newspaper industry is doing to our environment, I believe all publishers have an obligation to use recycled newsprint in lieu of virgin stock. I urge you to do so as soon and as often as possible. Information on companies that manufacture and supply recycled newsprint is included in the Paper Stock Dealers Directory (GIE Publishing, 4012 Bridge Ave., Cleveland, OH 44113, (800) 456–0707).

Thank you for your consideration.

Sincerely,

—
—
—
—

—
—
—
—

RE: An environmentally benign Christmas

Dear Editor:

Christmas is a time for rejoicing, sharing, forgiving, and enjoying spiritual peace. The last things most of us want to think about during the holidays are smog, acid rain, greenhouse warming, deforestation, water pollution, and the extinction of plant and animal species. Unfortunately, we can no longer afford to exclude these subjects from our holiday thoughts.

Christmas has become an enormous commercial circus. Merchants begin luring consumers earlier every year (this year they started long before Halloween) with massive campaigns designed to make us consume as much as possible. Most of us blithely comply, never realizing that our annual celebration also amounts to an assault on the environment.

Deforestation is a serious threat to the Earth's health. We are now cutting trees at such an appalling rate that virtually all our forests will be gone within a few decades if we do not change our ways. The clearing of forests often results in soil erosion, desertification of the land where trees once stood, and the extinction of the plant, animal, and insect species they harbored. And every time a tree is cut, the level of carbon dioxide in the Earth's atmosphere rises, exacerbating the greenhouse effect.

Paper is made (using processes that contribute to smog, acid rain, water pollution, and greenhouse warming) from fiber obtained by grinding trees into pulp. Millions of trees are cut each year to make the greeting cards, envelopes, stamps, boxes, packaging, labels, tissue, wrapping paper, and paper ribbon we discard soon after we receive them. We further contribute to deforestation every Christmas by cutting down enough Christmas trees in Canada and the U.S. to make a forest the size of Rhode Island. And, of course, we cut even more trees to make paper and wood gifts and cheery fires in our fireplaces.

Some ten thousand U.S. landfills have closed since 1979, and twenty-four hundred of the six thousand that remain will have to be closed by 1995 because they will be full. Nevertheless, after each Christmas, countless truckloads of discarded greeting cards, gift wrap, packaging, and trees are hauled to landfills, where they will occupy valuable space until they disintegrate and release more greenhouse gases into the air. Sprinkled throughout them are tons of plastic toys that were made from dwindling, nonrenewable supplies of petroleum using processes that generate air pollution and hazardous waste. The toys are broken a few days after Christmas, but once they are buried in landfills, they will not disintegrate for hundreds of years. Of course, they may be consumed by fire, which often occurs in landfills. In that case, many of them will emit toxic gases. Meanwhile, all garbage-disposal sites are sources of pollution, and the more waste they contain, the more likely they are to contaminate drinking water. According to an estimate made by the New York Department of Environmental Conservation in 1986, over two hundred landfills were polluting groundwater in New York alone. Thousands of disposal sites throughout the country have had to be closed because of pollution.

What can we do during the holidays to help save the Earth? We can buy recycled gift wrap and greeting cards (or not use any). We can buy live Christmas trees and plant them after Christmas. We can exchange gifts like memberships to environmental organizations, tree seedlings, solar battery chargers, and books dealing with environmental issues. We can avoid rain-forest beef, gifts that require batteries, and gifts made of teak, mahogany, rosewood, redwood, plastic, and unrecycled paper. We can turn our thermostats down a degree, put one less log on the fire, and make a special effort to recycle.

This year, let's sacrifice just a bit to give the Earth a holiday gift.

Sincerely,

—
—
—
—

PART II

Letters to Government Officials

Chapter 5

Letters to the President

"The quickest way to get things done is to go right to the top dog," my father taught me when I was a child. "Tell him who you are, look him straight in the eye, and tell him the truth."

You probably learned the same lesson, but, like me, you hold that knowledge in reserve, as a sort of ace in the hole, and use it only when something is really important.

This is one of those times.

So who is the "top dog"? The man who controls a large part of the bureaucracy and at least one of the purse strings of our country, who proposes and vetoes or signs into law federal legislation, and whose actions and words are heeded very carefully by the leaders of foreign governments: the President of the United States.

Most of us can't look the President in the eye and talk to him face-to-face, but all of us can send him mail. And we shouldn't be afraid to do so. The office of President deserves respect, but the President is not an unapproachable, godlike potentate who sits in the White House and hands down edicts, as many people seem to think. He is a man who is temporarily privileged to serve us because we elected him.

Like most public servants, the President pays attention to his mail—if not personally, at least by proxy—because he wants to keep abreast of your views and mine. He must know where the American public stands at all times. And regardless of what he may have done in the past, regardless of what he may have said during political campaigns,

press conferences, and State-of-the-Union addresses, if enough Americans tell him in writing that they want something done, chances are he will listen.

I would be delighted if the President were to receive letters asking for more environmental reform from every taxpayer in the country. Of course that will not happen, but perhaps this book will facilitate a lot more presidential letters by making it more convenient for Americans to send them. I hope so, because the President is not a mind reader; he cannot know what we want of him unless we tell him.

Below are a dozen preaddressed letters to the President concerning the environment. Like the letters in part I, they don't pretend to encompass every environmental problem or even all the major ones, but they point out actions the President can take to help make this planet a better, safer place for us to live, and to help insure that it will still be habitable when he and you and I pass it on to future generations.

The first letter, no. 36, asks the President to initiate or support efforts to develop clean, renewable energy sources like solar power and hydrogen at home and abroad.

Letter 37 asks for the return of tax incentives and/or the introduction of other economic measures to encourage conservation.

Letter 38 asks for the prevention of deforestation in the U.S. and around the world.

Letter 39 asks for the banning of certain chlorofluorocarbons (CFCs) and halons that are destroying the Earth's protective ozone layer.

Letter 40 suggests the establishment of economic incentives for recycling.

Letter 41 asks for the abandonment of nuclear-fission power plants and atomic weapons.

The Clean Air Act signed by President Bush in 1990 was a step in the right direction, but like most environmental legislation, it was too little too late. Letter 42 asks the President to adopt California's tough emission standards for automobiles and smokestacks across the U.S. and to urge foreign leaders to do the same in their countries.

Letter 43 asks for more responsible management of natural resources in the U.S. and elsewhere.

Letter 44 asks for stiffer penalties for polluters and suggests the resultant revenues be used to finance the development of nonpolluting alternatives.

Letter 45 asks for subsidies of organic farming, to be funded by taxes on mainstream farming.

Letter 46 asks the President to influence U.S. government offices and agencies to use clean, renewable energy sources in all government applications from military ships to office buildings.

Letter 47 asks the President to encourage all U.S. government offices and agencies to use less paper (and to use recycled paper and recycle the paper they use).

Later chapters include letters to officials in all levels of government, from the U.S. Senate to city and county executives.

The President
The White House
Washington, DC 20500

RE: Supporting renewable energy alternatives

Dear Mr. President:

I believe the Gulf War should serve as a cogent reminder that all nations
must wean themselves from oil dependence by developing renewable energy
alternatives. Because of our dependence on oil, the American public has
been forced to admit that the petroleum we import—nearly half of what we
use—leaves our economy helpless against the catastrophic effects of the
conflicts and whims of the Middle East, an area which has been unstable
throughout history and will likely remain so.

Increased domestic oil production cannot alter the fact that all the world's
oil will be depleted during the next century. Neither will it prevent the
thousands of oil spills that poison the Earth's waters each year, nor stop
greenhouse warming. Nor will it stop the acid rain that is killing forests
and fisheries and crops all over the world, or help the 76 million
Americans who must breathe air that fails to meet EPA standards.

But clean, renewable energy alternatives like photovoltaic, solar-thermal,
wind, small hydroelectric, geothermal, ocean-thermal, and tide energies can
combat all these problems simultaneously. Each of these energy sources is
available domestically in huge amounts. Each is virtually pollution-free
compared with fossil fuels. And when used in conjunction with water
electrolyzers, the energy produced by these alternative sources can be
converted into hydrogen, which creates almost no pollution at all when
burned, and can be used to fuel everything from power plants to furnaces
to automobiles.

In addition, renewable energy alternatives strengthen the security and
economy of the United States. They encourage decentralization of energy
production, leaving us less vulnerable to attacks on large refineries and
power plants. They create more local jobs, smoothing out the boom/bust
cycle that oil fosters. By lessening the amount of oil we import, they
reduce our trade deficit and bolster our economy. Finally, we can also
export the alternative technology.

The U.S. already possesses 100 percent of the technology needed to greatly expand its use of clean, renewable energy, but it has failed to do so because of simple economics. Hydrogen fuel from photovoltaic arrays would cost about two dollars for an amount equivalent to a gallon of gasoline, and electricity from most renewable sources is a bit more expensive than from coal-fired plants. But if downstream costs of fossil fuels are included in the equation (medical costs of treating people who breathe dirty air; losses of crops, fish, and buildings due to acid rain; the expense of protecting coastal areas from ocean levels that will rise because of the greenhouse effect; etc.), renewables are already cheaper than oil or coal.

Failure to include downstream costs in fossil-fuel prices inadvertently subsidizes global warming, acid rain, smog, the U.S. trade deficit, and continued dependence on foreign oil, and at the same time discourages the strengthening of our economy and security. And this situation is exacerbated by the fact that the U.S. government spends billions of dollars to protect Arab oil and subsidize nuclear-power research, while spending only a few million dollars to develop renewable energy. Yet, as the Chernobyl disaster and our growing stockpiles of nuclear waste have clearly demonstrated, downstream costs make nuclear power untenable.

In light of these conditions, I support tax advantages that balance the scale by favoring renewable energy development; tax levies that internalize the downstream costs of fossil fuels and nuclear power; and increased federal funding for renewable energy development. Incentives for renewable energy production should at least be equal to those now given to oil and nuclear power. I hope you will take appropriate measures to effect these changes and urge foreign leaders to do the same.

Thank you for your consideration.

Sincerely,

—
—
—
—

The President
The White House
Washington, DC 20500

RE: Economic incentives for conservation

Dear Mr. President:

The oil embargo of the 1970s triggered a number of energy conservation
measures in the United States. One such measure was the establishment of
income tax "energy credits," which have since expired. I believe the tax
credit idea was a good one. Because of it, a lot of Americans insulated
their homes, invested in solar collectors, etc., and helped to ameliorate the
"energy crisis" the U.S. was wrestling with at that time.

Now we face a much more severe crisis. Even before Saddam Hussein
threw the world's oil-based economy into turmoil, the U.S. trade deficit had
grown to gigantic proportions, largely because we import nearly half the
oil we use. But the consequences of that deficit, enormous though they
may be, pale in comparison to two other energy problems that face us
today. One is pollution. Smog, acid rain, and global warming—all largely
attributable to energy use—are rapidly destroying our environment. Many
experts agree that they have reached crisis stage around the world. The
other problem is oil depletion. The world's oil supply is, as you know,
projected to be virtually used up during the next century.

Climatologists, ecologists, and economists agree that energy conservation is
one of our most potent weapons against these problems. One way we can
conserve is to restore income tax credits for insulation, storm windows,
solar collectors, etc. Another is to provide incentives for the manufacture
and purchase of automobiles that get better mileage. It has been calculated
that improving the fuel efficiency of cars by 1.7 miles per gallon would save
more oil than we could ever get from Arctic drilling.

Of course, conservation alone cannot solve the environmental and energy
crises. Before that can be accomplished, clean, renewable energy sources
must also be developed, and deforestation must be stopped and reforestation
begun. But I believe that incentives like those I have outlined above are

relatively painless measures that will help enable us to avert economic and environmental disaster. I urge you to propose such incentives to Congress, and to encourage the leaders of other nations to consider following similar paths.

Thank you for your consideration.

Sincerely,

—
—
—
—

_____, 199_ #38

The President
The White House
Washington, DC 20500

RE: Stopping deforestation

Dear Mr. President:

I am very concerned about deforestation, and I think the United States
needs to do more to stop it.

Forests are vital to the health of our environment. They filter pollutants
out of the air—including the carbon dioxide that is the major cause of
global warming—and produce a large part of the oxygen we breathe. They
prevent erosion and flooding; stabilize humidity, temperature, rainfall, and
wind; shelter and feed plants, animals, and insects; and provide us with
shade, evaporative cooling, food, wood, paper, medicines, etc.

Yet, we are destroying the Earth's forests at an appalling rate. Tropical
rain forests, which shelter over half of all plant, animal, and insect species
and are the source of 40 percent of the Earth's atmospheric oxygen, are
being razed at the rate of five acres per minute (that's an area the size of
Ohio every year). By the year 2000, 80 percent of them may be gone.
Already, about three species of wildlife are becoming extinct every day, so
that entire ecosystems are threatened with collapse, and plants that may
have contained cures for cancer and AIDS will never be examined.

Americans are partially to blame. The U.S. imports about 800 million
pounds of paper from Brazil every year. Americans buy furniture made
from exotic tropical woods like teak, rosewood, and mahogany, the
harvesting of which destroys not only the lumber trees themselves, but
large areas of rain forest around them as well. We also buy beef from
ranches carved out of rain forests by slash-and-burn developers who don't
know or don't care that cattle grazing turns such ranches into eroding
deserts in only a few years. And our banks finance huge development
projects like road systems and dams that encourage further deforestation
in these fragile areas.

Our record at home is little better. Only 13 percent of the ancient forest growth in the Northern California-Oregon-Washington stand remains, and the Forest Service continues to indirectly subsidize the timber industry by selling timber on federal lands to commercial logging interests below cost—to the tune of $2 billion during the last decade. Some of this timber does not even stay in the U.S., but is shipped to Japan or other markets—often as whole logs, so that we do not even benefit from it in terms of processing jobs. Lumber and pulp industries across the U.S. habitually either clear-cut timber or fail to replace it properly. As a result, the forest ecosystems they leave behind may never recover.

If these trends are not mitigated, global warming and the extinction of species could escalate to catastrophic proportions. Rising sea levels, changing regional temperatures, and an increase in the frequency and severity of storms could bankrupt our economy and the economy of the world. And we might find that without the diversity of species that preserves the health of ecosystems, we may be incapable of sustaining our own food chain against insect swarms or other conditions we cannot foresee.

Deforestation must be moderated and reforestation begun. I hope you will propose trade restrictions that discourage the deforestation of other countries, propose tax advantages or other economic incentives that encourage reforestation in the U.S., insist that the Forest Service begin managing our national forests responsibly, and take any other actions necessary to reverse the current trends. And I hope you will urge foreign heads of state to institute their own programs to stop deforestation and foster reforestation in their countries.

Thank you for your consideration.

Sincerely,

The President
The White House
Washington, DC 20500

RE: Banning chlorofluorocarbons and halons

Dear Mr. President:

While billions of tax dollars and many lives are spent in the fight against
illegal drugs, chemicals that may ultimately be even more destructive are
being used legally. I refer to chlorofluorocarbons (or CFCs) and halons.

Scientists have now determined beyond all doubt that these chemicals are
responsible for the destruction of the Earth's protective ozone layer.
Studies show that as much as 6.2 percent of it is already gone, and the rate
of deterioration is accelerating because the amount of CFCs and halons in
the air is increasing, and each molecule of these chemicals can destroy up
to ten thousand molecules of ozone in the upper atmosphere.

As more of this protective layer disappears, more ultraviolet solar radiation
will leak through to the Earth's surface, damaging living things, including
man. Popular accounts have focused on the few thousand additional cases
of skin cancer we are likely to see as a short-term consequence, but the
problem is much graver than that. There will probably be increases in
cataracts and other signs of premature aging in man and other animals;
damage to immune systems; reductions in crop, timber, fish, and ranch
yields; an upset of the fragile marine ecology; a decrease in the size of plant
foliage; and eventually, a general decline, perhaps a total collapse, of the
entire biosphere.

As if that were not enough, these same chemicals are also responsible for
up to 20 percent of the greenhouse effect because they trap up to twenty
thousand times as much solar heat as does an equal amount of carbon
dioxide. And as greater volumes of them are released, that percentage—
and the subsequent rate of global warming—will grow dramatically. So,
even if efforts to replace fossil fuels with clean energy sources succeed, we
still will soon face rising sea levels and an increase in the frequency and
severity of storms unless we stop releasing these substances.

Of course, the U.S. government showed its recognition of the problem years ago when it banned the use of CFCs as aerosol propellants. But since that time their use has multiplied in other areas. And while some manufacturers and users have admitted the danger and voluntarily opted to discontinue their production and use, many have not. The electronics industry employs CFCs extensively as solvents. Hospitals use them as sterilants. Polystyrene and other plastic foams are full of them. Nearly every family in America now owns a refrigerator and/or air conditioner that uses them. And almost every CFC molecule will eventually seep into the air. Halons are less ubiquitous, but are used in fire extinguishers, and so are released not accidentally, but by design.

More benign substitutes for CFCs and halons have been identified for virtually every application. They are at present less convenient and/or initially more costly, but they are necessary—the price of not switching to them is unconscionable. Some plans have already been made to phase these substitutes in, but I believe these plans are too little too late. The situation is much too serious to allow the possible economic consequences to any particular business to get in the way of immediately substituting safer chemicals.

To help solve this potentially devastating problem, I urge you to work with the Congress, the EPA, and other agencies to ban the manufacture and distribution of CFCs and halons (not months or years from now, but right away), to impose new import restrictions that prevent them from entering the U.S., and to encourage the development of safer alternatives through economic incentives such as income tax breaks for manufacturers and consumers of such alternatives. And I ask that you try to influence foreign leaders to join you in your effort.

Thank you for your consideration.

Sincerely,

—
—
—
—

The President
The White House
Washington, DC 20500

RE: Establishing economic incentives for recycling

Dear Mr. President:

Like many U.S. citizens, I have grown very concerned about the environment. I believe we should be doing more to stop smog, acid rain, and greenhouse warming, not just for our own benefit, but for the benefit of our children and succeeding generations as well. And what better place to start than here in the United States, where disposable diapers, disposable razors, and disposable everything else have made us the most wasteful nation on Earth?

One of the quickest, cheapest ways to begin protecting the environment is to recycle paper. Every year, 850 million trees are cut to make the 50 million tons of paper Americans use. Much of it comes from the disappearing rain forests that until recently have harbored half the world's plant and animal species and have helped prevent a runaway greenhouse effect by absorbing carbon dioxide and producing 40 percent of the oxygen in our atmosphere. A lot of it comes from timber cut from our own federal lands. Virtually all of it ends up in our landfills, comprising nearly a third of the 154 million tons of garbage we generate yearly, and exacerbating the critical problem we face as more and more of our cities find they have no place left to dispose of solid wastes. Worse, the paper industry contributes greatly to smog, acid rain, and global warming because it is the largest single industrial user of fuel oil. And its processes use billions of gallons of our diminishing supplies of clean water and create large amounts of deadly dioxin.

Every ton of recycled paper saves 17 trees, 7,000 gallons of water, and the equivalent of 4,100 kilowatt-hours of electricity or 380 gallons of oil—enough to heat the average home for six months. It also causes 35 percent less water pollution and up to 95 percent less air pollution than paper made from virgin fiber, and keeps open as much landfill area as an average American uses in a year. And recycling creates jobs—five times as many people are needed to produce a ton of recycled paper as are needed to put out the same amount of paper made from virgin wood pulp.

But because of the U.S. Forest Service's policy of selling timber below cost (which indirectly subsidizes virgin-pulp production and discourages recycling), and because timber and pulp industries aren't required to include downstream costs in their prices for virgin pulp, recycled paper is having a hard time competing. Consumers are reluctant to buy recycled paper products because they are more expensive, so manufacturers are hesitant to use recycled paper. As a result, warehouses full of discarded newspapers sit waiting for buyers while the recycled paper industry struggles to grow.

I urge you to take action to save our environment by pushing for laws and tax advantages that favor manufacturers of recycled goods, and tax assessments that make the producers of virgin wood pulp responsible for the downstream consequences of their industry. And I ask that you urge the leaders of foreign governments to do the same in their own countries.

Thank you for your consideration.

Sincerely,

—
—
—
—

The President
The White House
Washington, DC 20500

RE: Abandoning nuclear power

Dear Mr. President:

Decades ago, when we decided to split atoms to meet the tremendous electricity demands of the future, we made two assumptions that were gravely in error. We assumed that nuclear accidents could be prevented and that science would soon find a safe way to dispose of nuclear wastes.

Nuclear accidents cannot be prevented, regardless of the amount of money spent on "fail-safe" backup systems. NRC documents show that more than thirty-three thousand mishaps, one thousand of which are considered significant, have occurred in U.S. power plants since the Three Mile Island incident in 1979. Testifying before the Energy and Power Subcommittee of the House Committee on Energy and Commerce in 1986, NRC Commissioner James Asseltine suggested a serious accident is likely to occur in the U.S. within two decades. The probability of a major core-melt during that period has been put at 45 percent by an NRC projection.

Such an accident would be catastrophic. The Chernobyl debacle in 1986 displaced 135,000 people from 179 villages; killed 31 people outright; irradiated so many that tens of thousands of cancer deaths, birth defects, and genetic mutations are expected; contaminated huge amounts of crops, livestock, and wildlife in several countries; and cost the Soviets $13 billion (including the loss of the power plant). An Atomic Energy Commission study done years ago estimated that a meltdown in the U.S. could injure 73,000 and kill 27,000, while causing $17 billion in property damage.

The so-called "inherently safe" reactors that have been proposed may be feasible to build decades from now, but even they are untenable, because we will still have no means of safely disposing of the spent fuel they will generate.

Such nuclear waste already presents serious problems. Since it stays dangerously radioactive for fifty thousand years and cannot be safely disposed of, voters who don't want it near them defeat dump-site proposals. As a result, it is only temporarily stored. By the year 2001, we may have seventy-two thousand tons of it. And we will also have enough low-level milling and mining waste to build a mound as high as a man's head from New York to Los Angeles.

If waste from fission reactors is dangerous, building the nuclear weapons they make possible is insane. As Carl Sagan and others have pointed out, a nuclear conflict cannot be won, because in addition to releasing deadly radiation, it would result in a "nuclear winter." According to the DOE, U.S. laboratories and plants that make nuclear weapons have released radioactive isotopes on at least 155 occasions (no one knows how many other instances have gone unreported). This pollution has probably caused thousands of cancers and birth defects in humans and an incalculable amount of damage to wildlife; and Congress has estimated that it will cost up to $200 billion over the next hundred years to clean it up. Nuclear weapons testing is credited with even greater damage. According to Dr. John Gofman, atomic testing has probably already condemned 1,116,000 people to developing lung cancer. Ironically, our nuclear weapons may already be obsolete; the threat of Soviet aggression, which they were designed to deter, seems to have disintegrated.

I am opposed to the exorbitant rates for electricity that nuclear plants charge. I resent being contaminated by nuclear waste. And I am sick of worrying that some human error or some software or hardware glitch might trigger a world-ending launch of nuclear warheads that nobody wants. I implore you to speed up the dismantling of stockpiled atomic weapons, to end the licensing of reactors, to urge the Congress to underwrite the development of clean, renewable energy sources to replace existing reactors, and to tell the other nuclear nations that they should do these same things.

Thank you for your consideration.

Sincerely,

—
—
—
—

The President
The White House
Washington, DC 20500

RE: Adopting tougher emission standards

Dear Mr. President:

In my opinion, the air pollution standards in the United States are neither
stringent enough, nor are they being enforced adequately. Although the
clean-air legislation introduced in 1990 was a step in the right direction, it
was too little too late. Ozone smog and acid rain are ruining our health
and destroying our forests, fisheries, and crops. According to the EPA, over
76 million Americans are breathing air that does not meet the clean-air
standards. And it is now clear that global warming is not a fanciful idea,
but a harsh reality.

Vehicles are a large part of the problem. According to the Department of
Transportation, the 140 million cars in the United States log 4 billion miles,
burn 200 million gallons of gasoline, and pump 4 billion pounds of carbon
dioxide into the air every day. They emit 20 percent of the fossil-fuel
carbon dioxide, 27 percent of the hydrocarbons, and 34 percent of the
nitrogen oxides that go into the atmosphere here. Trucks and buses are
even worse polluters than cars.

Chemical and oil plants and utilities are the sources of about half of our
nitrogen oxide and hydrocarbon pollutants. They also produce huge
amounts of carbon dioxide, as well as particulates, sulfur dioxide, and other
gases.

That these emissions must be reduced before smog, acid rain, and global
warming can be brought into check is without question. But so far our
efforts to do this have been tardy and unfocused. The U.S. is still widely
regarded as the world's most wasteful nation and its worst polluter.
During the 1980s, clean-air regulations that were inadequate to begin with,
were relaxed or disregarded time after time as government officials bowed
to the lobbying efforts of oil and chemical and automobile companies, and
placed the profitability of these companies above the health of the
environment and the American public.

It is now time to put those days behind us, and to insist on clean air. We can begin by adopting, nationwide, the tough emissions laws that the state of California has already pioneered. We can continue by studying Japan, which now has the strictest limits on emissions of any country, and by funneling the revenues received from penalties into the development of clean, renewable energy sources that will ultimately reduce emissions. And we can finish the job by sticking to our commitment, by enforcing the law, and by levying heavy fines against polluters and then collecting those fines—even forcing offenders out of business if necessary—rather than relaxing requirements to cater to special interests.

I hope you will take these steps to protect the inalienable right of every American—and of every living thing on this planet—to breathe clean air, and join the other countries of the world that have begun the fight against the ravages of air pollution. And I hope you will make use of every opportunity to encourage the leaders of other nations to act similarly in their own arenas.

Thank you for your consideration.

Sincerely,

—
—
—
—

The President
The White House
Washington, DC 20500

RE: Better management of natural resources

Dear Mr. President:

I am writing this letter to ask you to take measures that will stop—or at least slow—the destruction of natural resources, especially those on federal land.

I think most Americans are shocked when they learn that mining and oil-drilling operations are allowed in once-pristine wilderness areas, where they scar landscapes and upset ecosystems that took eons to evolve. They are saddened by the fact that Everglades National Park is losing its marvelous diversity of wildlife because its water supply has been diverted for commercial use. They are disgusted to see populations of loon, beaver, bear, and wolf threatened by the encroachment of tourists driving motorboats and snowmobiles in Voyageurs National Park. They are outraged to find the Forest Service actually encouraging devastation of our national forests by cutting roads through them and then selling timber to commercial loggers at a loss of half a billion dollars per year.

These are just a few of many examples of the myopia and subsequent mismanagement characteristic of U.S. government efforts to manage natural resources. Because of our lack of foresight in the past, the Great Plains that once thundered under the hooves of millions of bison are now silent; 87 percent of the magnificent ancient forests that once covered the Northwest have been felled and their ecosystems changed forever; and an alarming number of streams and lakes are now lifeless due to pollution. And now we are discovering that even our healthiest national parks are incapable of sustaining the ecosystems indigenous to them in the long term because they are not large enough and are not surrounded by the buffer zones necessary to protect them from human influence.

If we are to pass on any natural resources at all to future generations, we must stop thinking of our country and the rest of the Earth in terms of how much ore and lumber and water we can strip from them. We must begin thinking of them as fragile, complex, interconnected systems, sensitive to all foreign stimuli, and worthy of preservation.

I want you to know that I support movement away from present
government policies that allow politicians to cater to commercial interests
at the expense of our natural resources, and toward new ones that place
preservation first. I support the restructuring of our unwieldy
bureaucracy so that it can look at natural resources from a much wider
perspective, and so that it can ensure conservation rather than allowing
resources to be plundered. I support the abandonment of unconscionably
expensive military programs so that more funds can be diverted toward
sound, comprehensive management of natural resources. It is my hope
that you will use your influence to bring these changes about in the U.S.,
and that you will encourage your colleagues from other countries to
promote similar programs abroad.

Thank you for your consideration.

Sincerely,

The President
The White House
Washington, DC 20500

RE: Stiffer fines for oil spills, toxic dumping, etc.

Dear Mr. President:

About 700,000 tons of toxic waste are generated in the United States every day—enough to fill the New Orleans Superdome 15,000 times a year. Some of it is spilled or illegally dumped, as are tens of thousands of other hazardous substances that are not considered wastes. Each year brings with it more horror stories like the ones from Love Canal and Three Mile Island and Prince William Sound. Every week, more oil spills contaminate our waterways, more industrial effluent pours into our streams, more radioactivity is released into our air, more gasoline leaks into our drinking water from underground tanks, more toxic chemicals are spilled on our highways, and so on.

Although the Environmental Protection Agency is supposed to cope with the problem, it cannot. It operates on a yearly budget of $8.5 billion, but it would take $30 billion to clean up just the sites that have already been identified (ignoring those that are yet to be reported). Some states have their own regulations, but many of these are inadequate. The trouble is not that more taxes need to be appropriated, but that federal policies and regulations need to be rewritten.

At present, EPA regulations allow generators of less than one hundred kilograms of hazardous waste per month to dispose of it as if it were ordinary garbage, without paying any fines at all. Companies whose trucks, trains, or ships are involved in accidents are often not charged for spills of oil or other hazardous substances. Industrial polluters are usually simply asked to clean up their messes. If they refuse, they may or may not be prosecuted. If judges rule against them, they may or may not be forced to comply, but only after lengthy appeals, during which many continue to pollute. Occasionally one is charged a fine that amounts to a slap on the wrist.

This must be changed. Polluters should be held responsible for their actions. Offenders should immediately be enjoined from further discharges and heavily fined. If they refuse to comply, they should be jailed and charged, and their assets confiscated for payment of their fines, just as they would be had they refused to pay their income taxes. Revenues from such fines should be used to pay not only cleanup costs, but also the expense of developing alternative products that are not hazardous.

What I ask of you is that you work with the EPA, the Congress, the Justice Department, and the various state governments to shift the burden of preventing and cleaning up hazardous spills and toxic dump sites away from taxpayers and toward polluters, and to place on polluters the additional burden of financing the development of alternate substances that are not hazardous.

Thank you for your consideration.

Sincerely,

—
—
—
—

The President
The White House
Washington, DC 20500

RE: Economic incentives for organic farming

Dear Mr. President:

This year, Americans will spend huge sums of money to contaminate the
Earth with 2.7 billion pounds of pesticides in an effort to poison unwanted
insects, fungi, etc. Some fifty thousand varieties of pesticides will be used,
most of which have never been tested. Of those that have been tested, over
one hundred ingredients used in them are suspected of causing cancer,
birth defects, and/or gene mutations. And many of these ingredients will
be absorbed into the food we eat and/or the water we drink. The EPA has
already found seventy-four pesticides in the groundwater of thirty-eight
states in the U.S.—the drinking water of half the American population.

Ironically, though they weaken the soil by attacking earthworms and
microorganisms that normally keep it healthy, and though they sicken and
kill birds, animals, fish, insects, and people, these pesticides lack real
effectiveness. Many pests have developed an immunity to them. Over 70
types of fungi and 440 types of mites and insects are resistant to
pesticides. As a result, farmers lose about a third of their crops to pests,
just as they did before pesticides were introduced.

Meanwhile, other chemicals exacerbate the situation. Artificial chemical
fertilizers "rev up" plant growth to produce faster yields, but also cause
algae blooms that kill fish and other aquatic life in waterways, contaminate
drinking water, become absorbed into foods, etc. Preservatives retard the
growth of harmful bacteria, but they also retard beneficial bacteria, and
they themselves may cause cancer. Mixed chemicals can result in a
synergism (combined they can be more deleterious than individually).

Consequently, American food products are often not "good, wholesome food"
at all, but a chemical soup containing herbicides, fungicides, insecticides,
rodenticides, chemical fertilizers, preservatives, flavor enhancers,
emulsifiers, and so on any one of which may be harmful to the people who
consume them.

A 1988 Louis Harris poll found that 84 percent of American adults would rather buy organic foods that do not contain these contaminants. Were they to do so, they would improve the environment and the economy as well as their health. Aside from not eroding and wearing out soil and polluting water with pesticides and fertilizers, organic farms require less mechanization, which means less of the air pollution that causes smog, acid rain, and greenhouse warming. They also usually sell more of their products to local markets, so they require less transportation, which further reduces air pollution. And because weeds and bugs must be hand-picked, organic farms provide more jobs than equivalent mainstream farms.

Although organic farming is growing in popularity, it is having trouble competing because the downstream costs of normal agribusiness (the costs of health care for people dying of chemical-induced cancers, the amount of damage done to wildlife, the expense of maintaining buildings attacked by acid rain, etc.) are not included in mainstream food prices. Because of this inequity—and only because of it—organic foods (which have little or no such downstream costs, but which require more labor to produce), carry higher checkout price tags. So most consumers still choose mainstream items.

In light of these facts, I believe it is your duty as President to call for federal subsidies of organic foods, with funding to come from taxes that force the internalization of the downstream costs of nonorganic foods. This would remove hidden subsidies that are now underwriting destructive mainstream farming.

Thank you for your consideration.

Sincerely,

—
—
—
—

The President
The White House
Washington, DC 20500

<u>RE</u>: Use of renewable energy by the government

Dear Mr. President:

I believe the U.S. government should begin employing energy conservation
measures and clean, renewable energy sources like solar power, wind
power, and electrolytic hydrogen in each new government installation,
whether it be a ship at sea, an air force base, or an office building.

The Chernobyl disaster and the insoluble problem of what to do with
nuclear wastes have proven that nuclear fission is too dangerous. Fossil
fuels cause smog, acid rain, and global warming, and will be depleted
within a few decades. Both of these energy sources threaten to virtually
destroy our environment, and both require huge, centralized power-
generation stations to produce electricity (and/or fuel), which are easy
targets for terrorist or enemy attacks. And neither provides a stable
foundation for our economy.

But clean, renewable energy alternatives like photovoltaic, solar-thermal,
wind, small hydroelectric, geothermal, ocean-thermal, and tide energies can
never be depleted. They produce virtually no pollution. When used in
conjunction with water electrolyzers, the energy produced by each of these
alternative sources can be converted into hydrogen, which produces almost
no pollution at all when burned, and which can be used to fuel everything
from power plants to furnaces to automobiles. And they encourage
decentralization, even complete energy independence—which translates
into better security and a hedge against inflation.

The U.S. government already possesses all the technology it needs to begin
using clean, renewable energy, but it has failed to do so except in
specialized applications like satellites and remote weather stations because
of simple economics. Hydrogen fuel from photovoltaic arrays would cost
about two dollars for an amount equivalent to a gallon of gasoline, and
electricity from most renewable sources is a bit more expensive than from
coal-fired plants. But if downstream costs of fossil fuels and nuclear

fission are included in the equation (medical costs of treating people who breathe dirty air; losses of crops, fish, and buildings to acid rain and fallout; the expense of protecting Arab oil and of protecting coastal areas from ocean levels that will rise because of the greenhouse effect; etc.), renewables are already more cost-effective.

Since the government ends up paying a large percentage of these downstream costs, it actually loses money by not using more renewable energy sources (and compromises its own security, the environment, public health, and the health of the American economy at the same time). By not using more renewables, it actually subsidizes smog, acid rain, global warming, radioactive contamination, dependence on foreign oil, the depletion of natural resources, mass migrations during oil booms, and the escalating U.S. trade deficit.

The most expeditious way to remedy this situation is to immediately begin including clean, renewable energy use in all new government designs. For instance, architects should be instructed to include solar collectors, photovoltaic modules, and wind generators in their designs for new government buildings; U.S. Navy ship designs should include solar cells and hydrogen engines; coastal military bases should begin harnessing tide energy; and so on.

I urge you to take any action necessary to ensure that the U.S. government begins, right away, the inevitable process of phasing in clean, renewable energy and phasing out fossil fuels and nuclear power, rather than waiting until it is forced, by crises, to do so hastily. And I hope you will make use of every opportunity you have to help or encourage other governments do the same.

Thank you for your consideration.

Sincerely,

—
—
—
—

The President
The White House
Washington, DC 20500

RE: More use of recycled paper by the government

Dear Mr. President:

I urge you to direct all government offices to reduce the amount of paper they use, to buy more recycled paper (preferably "minimum impact" off-white paper), and to recycle more of their waste paper.

The United States consumes more paper than any other nation—more than fifty million tons per year. Most of it is made from virgin wood pulp through processes which use, for every ton of paper, 28 million Btus of energy, 24,000 gallons of water, 360 pounds of salt cake, 216 pounds of lime, 76 pounds of soda ash, and 17 trees, and produce 176 pounds of solid waste and 120 pounds of air and water pollutants (including deadly dioxin and furans). This not only depletes valuable natural resources, but also contributes to erosion, smog, acid rain, global warming, deforestation, desertification, and the extinction of plant, animal, and insect species. And because we use most paper only once and discard it, paper occupies a third of our overcrowded landfill space.

All of these problems can be addressed simultaneously and forcefully by simply conserving and recycling paper. Recycling consumes no trees and up to 60 percent less water and 70 percent less energy; causes 35 percent less water pollution and up to 95 percent less air pollution; and creates five times as many jobs as virgin pulp processing. Since it is the bleaching process that generates dioxin when paper is made from virgin pulp, recycling, which requires less bleaching, creates less dioxin—and the production of minimum impact off-white recycled paper is virtually dioxin-free.

That recycling is cost-effective is undeniable. Industries have profited from it for years, and now many municipalities and several states, awakened to the fact that recycling is the most efficient waste-management option available, have followed their lead. Maryland, for instance, has saved enough energy by recycling to heat ten thousand homes for a year.

Despite its advantages, though, recycled paper struggles to compete because of lack of consumer demand. Even though it would be cheaper, were below-cost Forest Service timber sales discontinued and downstream costs of virgin pulp pollution internalized, its market price makes it appear more expensive to the consumer. Consequently, consumers are reluctant to buy it, so manufacturers are reluctant to use it—with the result that concerned citizens often collect more wastepaper than can be used, while sales of recycled products remain slow.

What is needed to break this impasse is a large demand for recycled paper, and I think the government should provide that demand. The U.S. government is by far the world's largest user of paper. The Congressional Record alone consumes a staggering amount of paper, which is in turn dwarfed by the billions of tax forms, brochures, letters, and other documents generated by government offices. Some of these are already printed on recycled paper, but a huge number are not. I believe this is a situation that the government has an obligation to correct. I believe there is no good reason for not eventually using recycled paper in every U.S. government application, from army toilet tissue to White House stationery, if it will help save the world's forests and slow pollution and global warming.

While more revenue would initially be required for the procurement of recycled paper than is now budgeted, the extra outlay should be more than offset by revenues from recycling government wastepaper, and from savings in health care payments for the effects of pollution, reforestation expenses, timber industry subsidies, support for the jobless, crop, forest, and fishery losses due to acid rain, dioxin cleanups, etc.

Thank you for your consideration.

Sincerely,

—
—
—
—

Chapter 6

Letters to U.S. Senators and Representatives

While the President has a great deal of power, it is Congress that makes the laws—and approves the budget. And regardless of how dedicated an environmentalist the President becomes after reading our letters (millions of them, I hope!), a Congress dedicated to the status quo can prove an insurmountable obstacle to him.

So, although we have helped to save the Earth by sending all those letters to our friend in the White House, our job is far from complete. Before we are likely to see the federal legislation we want, we must also convince the Senate and the House of Representatives we mean business.

Toward that end, this chapter consists of a dozen letters to congresspersons, all designed to convey just how important we consider environmental action to be.

If you are reading this book straight through, these letters will seem redundant because they closely parallel the presidential letters in Chapter 5. This repetition is necessary because of the same checks and balances that make our system of government desirable. We are most likely to get the President and Congress to agree on legislation if we give both of them exactly the same information.

Since two senators and a representative represent you directly, you may wish to copy these letters. Please read the requirements on the copyright page of this book before doing so.

The name of every member of the 102nd Congress (established November 6, 1990) is listed in appendix B of this book. To find your senators and representative, first locate the name of your state in the alphabetical listings. Then, using letter no. 0 as a guide, address your letters this way:

The Honorable [full name of senator]
U.S. Senate
Washington, DC 20510

The Honorable [representative's full name]
U.S. House of Representatives
Washington, DC 20515

Greetings should be written in this form:

Dear Senator [senator's last name]:
Dear Congressman [representative's last name]:
Dear Congresswoman [representative's last name]:

If you are unable to determine the gender of a congressperson, you may use:

Dear Representative [representative's last name]:

If you don't know what district you live in or who represents you, you can find out by asking the reference librarian at your library to look in the *Congressional Staff Directory* or by calling your county courthouse, city hall, or a voter organization like the League of Women Voters.

If you think members of Congress disregard letters from constituents, you are wrong. Some of them get pretty cocky sometimes, but most never forget that voters have the power to remove them from office. Even though many don't read most of their mail personally, they hire staff people who do and who keep them abreast of how many of their constituents want this and how many want that.

So keep sending those cards and letters...and don't forget to register and vote!

—
—
—

—

RE: Supporting renewable energy alternatives

Dear

I believe all nations should wean themselves from dependence on oil by
developing renewable energy sources. The Gulf War reinforced this idea.
Because of it, the American public was forced to admit that the petroleum
we import—nearly half of what we use—lays our economy bare to the
catastrophic effects of conflicts and whims in the Middle East, a region
which has been unstable throughout history and will likely remain so.

Increased domestic oil production cannot alter the fact that all the world's
oil will be depleted during the next century. Neither will it prevent the
thousands of oil spills that poison the Earth's waters each year, nor stop
global warming. Nor will it stop the acid rain that is killing forests and
fisheries and crops all over the world, or help the 76 million Americans
who must breathe air that fails to meet EPA standards.

But clean, renewable energy alternatives (photovoltaic, solar thermal, wind,
small hydroelectric, geothermal, ocean thermal, and tide energies) can
combat all these problems simultaneously. Each of them is available
domestically in huge amounts. Each is virtually pollution-free compared
with fossil fuels. And when used in conjunction with water electrolyzers,
the energy produced by these alternative sources can be converted into
hydrogen, which produces almost no pollution at all when burned and
which can be used to fuel everything from power plants to furnaces to
automobiles.

In addition, renewables strengthen the security and economy of the United
States. They encourage decentralization of energy production, leaving us
less vulnerable to attacks on large refineries and power plants. They
create more local jobs, smoothing out the boom/bust cycle that oil fosters.
And they also reduce our trade deficit by lessening the amount of oil we
import, thereby bolstering our economy.

The U.S. already possesses 100 percent of the technology needed to greatly expand its use of clean, renewable energy, but it has failed to do so because of simple economics. Hydrogen fuel from photovoltaic arrays would cost about two dollars for an amount equivalent to a gallon of gasoline, and electricity from most renewable sources is a bit more expensive than from coal-fired plants. But if the downstream costs of fossil fuels are included in the equation (medical costs of treating people who breathe dirty air; losses of crops, fish, and buildings due to acid rain; the expense of protecting coastal areas from ocean levels that will rise because of the greenhouse effect; etc.), renewables are already cheaper than oil or coal.

Failure to internalize downstream costs in fossil-fuel prices inadvertently subsidizes global warming, acid rain, smog, the U.S. trade deficit, and continued dependence on foreign oil, and at the same time discourages the strengthening of our economy and security. And this situation is exacerbated by the fact that the U.S. government spends billions of dollars to protect Arab oil and subsidize nuclear-power research, while spending only a few million dollars to develop renewable energy. Yet, as the Chernobyl disaster and our growing stockpiles of nuclear wastes have clearly demonstrated, downstream costs make nuclear power untenable.

In light of these conditions, I urge you to introduce or support legislation providing tax advantages and/or increased federal funding for renewable energy production at least equal to the incentives now given to fossil fuels and nuclear power, and/or tax levies that internalize the downstream costs of fossil fuels and nuclear power.

Thank you for your consideration.

Sincerely,

——
——
——
——

—
—
—
—

<u>RE: Establishing economic incentives for conservation</u>

Dear

I am a taxpayer interested in reducing the U.S. trade deficit and protecting the environment. I am writing to urge you to introduce or support legislation that restores the expired income tax "energy credits" that once allowed many Americans to insulate their homes, or that establishes other economic incentives for energy conservation.

Even before Saddam Hussein threw the world's oil-based economy into turmoil in 1990, the U.S. trade deficit had grown to gigantic proportions, largely because we import nearly half the oil we use. But the consequences of that deficit, enormous though they may be, pale in comparison to two other energy problems that face us today. One is pollution. Smog, acid rain, and global warming—all largely attributable to energy use—are destroying our environment. Many experts agree that they have reached crisis stage around the world. The other problem is oil depletion. The world's oil supply is projected to be virtually used up during the next century.

Climatologists, ecologists, and economists agree that energy conservation is one of our most potent weapons against these problems. One way we can conserve is to restore income tax credits for insulation, storm windows, solar collectors, etc. Another is to provide incentives for the manufacture and purchase of automobiles that get better mileage. It has been calculated that improving the fuel efficiency of cars by 1.7 miles per gallon would save more oil than we could ever get from Arctic drilling.

Of course, conservation alone cannot solve the environmental and energy crises. Before that can be accomplished, clean, renewable energy sources must also be developed, and deforestation must be stopped and reforestation begun. But I believe that incentives like those I have suggested above are relatively painless measures that will help us to avert economic and environmental disaster.

Thank you for your consideration.

Sincerely,

—
—
—
—

—
—
—
—

RE: Stopping deforestation

Dear

I believe federal legislation is needed to discourage deforestation and encourage reforestation in the United States and throughout the world.

Forests are vital to the health of our environment. They filter pollutants out of the air, including the carbon dioxide that is the major cause of global warming. They produce a large part of the oxygen we breathe. They prevent erosion and flooding; stabilize the atmosphere; shelter and feed other living things; and provide us with shade, evaporative cooling, food, wood, paper, medicines, etc.

Despite all of this, we are destroying the Earth's forests at an appalling rate. Tropical rain forests, which harbor over half of all plant, animal, and insect species and are the source of 40 percent of the Earth's atmospheric oxygen, are being razed at the rate of five acres per minute (that's an area the size of Ohio every year). By the year 2000, 80 percent of them may be gone. Already, about three species of wildlife are becoming extinct every day, threatening entire ecosystems with collapse, and plants that may have contained cures for cancer and AIDS will never be examined.

Americans are partially to blame. The U.S. imports about 800 million pounds of paper from Brazil every year. Americans buy furniture made from exotic tropical woods like teak, rosewood, and mahogany, the harvesting of which destroys large areas of rain forest. We also buy beef from ranches carved out of rain forests by slash-and-burn developers who don't know or don't care that cattle grazing turns such ranches into eroding deserts in only a few years. And our banks finance huge development projects like road systems and dams that encourage further deforestation in these fragile areas.

Our record at home is little better. Only 13 percent of the ancient forest growth in the Northern California-Oregon-Washington stand remains, and the Forest Service continues to indirectly subsidize the timber industry by selling timber on federal lands to commercial logging interests below cost—to the tune of $2 billion over the last decade. Some of this timber does not even stay in the U.S., but is shipped to Japan or other markets—often as whole logs, so that we do not even benefit from it in terms of processing jobs. Lumber and pulp industries across the U.S. habitually either clear-cut timber or fail to replace it properly. As a result, the forest ecosystems they leave behind may never recover.

If these trends are not mitigated, global warming and the extinction of species could escalate to catastrophic proportions. Rising sea levels, changing regional temperatures, and an increase in the frequency and severity of storms could bankrupt our economy and the economy of the world. And we might find that without the diversity of species that preserves the health of ecosystems, we cannot sustain our own food chain against insect swarms or other conditions we cannot foresee.

I urge you to introduce or back trade restrictions designed to discourage deforestation, to support the provision of tax advantages or other economic incentives that encourage reforestation, and to foster legislation that forces the Forest Service to manage our national forests more responsibly.

Thank you for your consideration.

Sincerely,

—
—
—
—

—
—
—
—

RE: Banning chlorofluorocarbons and halons

Dear

If attempts by members of Congress to ban flag burning and street drugs and obscene art are indications of concern for the welfare of the American public, then I suggest the time for a bill banning certain chemicals known as chlorofluorocarbons (or CFCs) and halons is long overdue.

As you are no doubt aware, scientists have now determined beyond all doubt that these chemicals are responsible for the destruction of the Earth's protective ozone layer. Studies show that as much as 6.2 percent of it is already gone, and the rate of its deterioration is accelerating because the amount of CFCs and halons in the air is increasing, and each molecule of them can destroy up to ten thousand molecules of ozone in the upper atmosphere.

As more of the protective ozone layer disappears, more ultraviolet solar radiation will leak through to the Earth's surface, damaging living things, including humans. Popular accounts have focused on the few thousand additional cases of skin cancer we are likely to see as a short-term consequence, but the problem is much more grave than that. There will probably be increases in cataracts and other signs of premature aging in humans and other animals; damage to immune systems; reductions in crop, timber, fish, and ranch yields; an upset of the fragile marine ecology; a decrease in the size of plant foliage; and eventually, a general decline, perhaps a total collapse, of the Earth's entire biosphere.

As if that were not enough, these same chemicals are responsible for up to 20 percent of the greenhouse effect because they trap up to twenty thousand times as much solar heat as does an equal amount of carbon dioxide. And as greater volumes of them are released, that percentage— and the subsequent rate of global warming—will grow dramatically. So, even if efforts to replace fossil fuels with clean, renewable energy sources succeed, we still will soon face rising sea levels and an increase in the frequency and severity of storms unless we stop the emission of these substances.

Of course, the use of CFCs as aerosol propellants was banned in the U.S. years ago. But since that time their use has multiplied in other areas. And while some manufacturers and users have admitted the dangers and voluntarily opted to quit buying and selling them, many have not. The electronics industry employs CFCs extensively as solvents. Hospitals use them as sterilants. Polystyrene and other plastic foams are full of them. Nearly every family in America now owns a refrigerator and/or air conditioner that uses them. And almost every CFC molecule will eventually seep into the air. Halons are less ubiquitous than CFCs, but are used in fire extinguishers, and so are released not accidentally, but by design.

More benign substitutes for CFCs and halons have been identified for virtually every application. These alternatives are at present less convenient and/or initially more costly, but they are necessary—the price of not switching to them is unconscionable. Some plans have already been made to phase these alternatives in, but I believe these plans are too little too late. The situation is much too serious to allow the possible economic consequences to any particular business to get in the way of immediately substituting safer chemicals.

To help solve this potentially devastating problem and protect our environment, I ask that you introduce or support bills that ban the manufacture and distribution of CFCs and halons (not months or years from now, but right away), that impose new import restrictions to prevent them from entering the U.S., and that encourage the development of safer alternatives through economic incentives such as income tax breaks for manufacturers and consumers of such alternatives.

Thank you for your consideration.

Sincerely,

—

—

—

—

—
—
—
—

RE: Establishing economic incentives for recycling

Dear

Please count me among those of your constituents who want new federal legislation covering virgin wood pulp production and the manufacture of recycled goods.

Recycling more of the 50 million tons of paper Americans use each year is one of the quickest, cheapest ways to ease the environmental crisis that faces us today.

Many of the 850 million trees that are pulped each year to make that paper are taken from the disappearing rain forests that until recently have harbored half the world's land species and have helped prevent a runaway greenhouse effect by absorbing carbon dioxide and producing 40 percent of the oxygen in our atmosphere. Many others are cut from our own federal lands. Wherever they come from, cutting trees down contributes to deforestation, erosion, and global warming.

Most of the paper produced is used once and discarded. It comprises nearly a third of the 154 million tons of garbage we generate yearly, and complicates the critical problem we face as more and more of our landfills overflow.

Worse, the paper industry contributes greatly to smog, acid rain, and global warming because it is the largest single industrial user of fuel oil. And its processes use billions of gallons of our diminishing supplies of clean water and create large amounts of deadly dioxin.

Recycling is much better for the environment. Every ton of recycled paper saves 17 trees, 7,000 gallons of water, and the equivalent of 4,100 kilowatt-hours of electricity or 380 gallons of oil—enough to heat the average home for six months. It also causes 35 percent less water pollution and up to 95 percent less air pollution, and keeps open as much landfill area as an average American uses in a year. And recycling creates jobs—five times as many people are needed to produce a ton of recycled paper as are needed to put out the same amount of paper made from virgin wood pulp.

But the recycled paper industry is struggling against unfair odds. The U.S. Forest Service sells timber below cost to commercial pulp operations, indirectly subsidizing virgin pulp production and discouraging recycling. And timber and pulp industries aren't required to include downstream costs in their prices for virgin pulp (costs like the money spent to clean up dioxin, restore lakes ruined by acid rain, care for people suffering pollution-related respiratory illness, etc.); consequently, prices for virgin pulp paper are artificially kept lower than recycled paper prices. Consumers are reluctant to pay the higher prices for recycled paper, and manufacturers respond by being hesitant to use it. As a result, warehouses full of discarded newspapers sit waiting for buyers while trees continue to fall.

I urge you to take action to save our environment by giving the recycled paper industry a fighting chance to compete with traditional paper producers. Please introduce or support tax incentives that favor manufacturers of recycled goods, and tax assessments that make the producers of virgin wood pulp responsible for the downstream consequences of their industry.

Thank you for your consideration.

Sincerely,

—
—
—
—

—

—

—

—

RE: Abandoning nuclear power

Dear

Like millions of other Americans, I am opposed to nuclear arms and nuclear power plants.

Decades ago, when we decided to split atoms to meet the electricity demands of the future, we gambled the safety of the American public on two guesses—that nuclear accidents could be prevented, and that science would soon find a safe way to dispose of nuclear wastes. And we lost.

Nuclear accidents cannot be prevented, regardless of how many billions are spent on "fail-safe" backup systems. NRC documents show that more than thirty-three thousand of them have occurred in domestic power plants since the 1979 incident at Three Mile Island. A thousand of these are considered significant. Testifying before the Energy and Power Subcommittee of the House Committee on Energy and Commerce in 1986, NRC Commissioner James Asseltine suggested a serious accident is likely in the U.S. within two decades. The probability of a major core-melt during that period has been put at 45 percent by an NRC projection.

Such an accident would be catastrophic. The Chernobyl debacle in 1986 displaced 135,000 people from 179 villages; killed 31 people outright; irradiated so many that tens of thousands of cancer deaths, birth defects, and genetic mutations are expected; contaminated huge amounts of crops, livestock, and wildlife in several countries; and cost the Soviets $13 billion (including the loss of the power plant). An Atomic Energy Commission study done years ago estimated that a meltdown in the U.S. could injure 73,000 and kill 27,000, while causing $17 billion in property damage.

So-called "inherently safe" reactors that have been proposed may be feasible to build decades from now, but even they are untenable; we will still have no safe means of disposing of the spent fuel they will generate.

Such waste already presents serious problems. Since it stays dangerously radioactive for fifty thousand years and cannot be safely disposed of, voters who don't want it near them defeat dump site proposals. So, it is only temporarily stored. By the year 2001, we may have seventy-two thousand tons of it. And by that time we will also have enough low-level milling and mining waste to build a mound as high as a man's head from New York to Los Angeles.

If waste from fission reactors is dangerous, building the nuclear weapons they make possible is insane. As Carl Sagan and others have pointed out, a nuclear conflict cannot be won, because in addition to releasing deadly radiation, it would result in a "nuclear winter." According to the DOE, U.S. laboratories and plants that make nuclear weapons have released radioactive isotopes on at least 155 occasions (no one knows how many other instances have gone unreported). This pollution has probably caused thousands of cancers and birth defects in humans and an incalculable amount of damage to wildlife; and Congress has estimated that it will cost up to $200 billion over the next hundred years to clean it up. Nuclear weapons testing is credited with even greater damage. According to Dr. John Gofman, atomic testing has probably already condemned 1,116,000 people to developing lung cancer. Ironically, our nuclear weapons may already be obsolete; the threat of Soviet aggression, which they were designed to deter, seems to have disintegrated.

Let's not wait until tens of thousands of Americans are killed by a meltdown, or tens of millions by a nuclear war triggered by a software or hardware malfunction. Let's put a stop to nuclear power now. I urge you to vote for legislation that speeds up the dismantling of atomic weapons stockpiles; ends the licensing of reactors; underwrites the development of clean, renewable energy sources to replace existing reactors; and bans the importation or exportation of atomic arms and reactors.

Thank you for your consideration.

Sincerely,

___

___

___

___

—
—
—
—

RE: Adopting tougher emission standards

Dear

In my opinion, the air pollution standards in the United States are neither stringent enough, nor adequately enforced. Ozone smog and acid rain are ruining our health and destroying our forests, fisheries, and crops. According to the EPA, over 76 million Americans are breathing air that does not meet the clean-air standards. And it is now clear that global warming is not a fanciful idea, but a harsh reality.

Vehicles are a large part of the problem. According to the Department of Transportation, the 140 million cars in the United States log 4 billion miles, burn 200 million gallons of gasoline, and pump 4 billion pounds of carbon dioxide into the air every day. They emit 20 percent of the fossil-fuel carbon dioxide, 27 percent of the hydrocarbons, and 34 percent of the nitrogen oxides that go into the atmosphere here. Trucks and buses are even worse polluters than cars.

Chemical and oil plants and utilities are the sources of about half our nitrogen oxide and hydrocarbon pollutants. They also produce huge amounts of carbon dioxide, as well as particulates, sulfur dioxide, and other gases.

That these emissions must be reduced before smog, acid rain, and global warming can be brought into check is without question. But so far our efforts to do this have been tardy and unfocused. The U.S. is still widely regarded as the world's most wasteful nation and its worst polluter. During the 1980s, clean-air regulations were relaxed or disregarded time after time as government officials bowed to the demands of oil, chemical, and automobile companies, placing the profitability of these companies above the health of the environment and the American public. And clean-air legislation introduced in 1990, though a step in the right direction, was too little too late.

It is now time to put those days behind us, to take heed of the Montreal Protocol, and to insist on clean air. I urge you to introduce or support legislation, drafted in such a way that it can be stringently enforced once it becomes law, that adopts for the entire U.S. the tough emission standards the state of California has already pioneered, and that stipulates stiff penalties be paid for violations and funneled into the development of renewable energy sources that will ultimately reduce emissions. And I encourage you to build into that legislation safeguards to prevent its requirements from being relaxed to satisfy lobbyists representing the business sector, as has happened with past clean-air bills.

I hope you will take these steps to protect the inalienable right of every American—and of every living thing on this planet—to breathe clean air, and to join the other countries of the world that have already begun the fight against the ravages of air pollution.

Thank you for your consideration.

Sincerely,

___

___

___

___

—
—
—
—

RE: Better management of natural resources

Dear

I think most Americans are shocked when they learn that mining and oil drilling operations are allowed in once-pristine wilderness areas, where they scar landscapes and upset ecosystems that took eons to evolve. They are saddened by the fact that Everglades National Park is losing its marvelous diversity of species because its water supply has been diverted for commercial use. They are disgusted to see populations of loon, beaver, bear, and wolf threatened by the encroachment of tourists driving motorboats and snowmobiles in Voyageurs National Park. They are outraged to find the Forest Service actually encouraging devastation of our national forests by cutting roads through them and then selling timber to commercial loggers at a loss of half a billion dollars per year.

These are just a few of many examples of the myopia and subsequent mismanagement characteristic of U.S. government efforts to manage natural resources. Because of our lack of foresight in the past, the Great Plains that once thundered under the hooves of millions of bison are now silent; 87 percent of the magnificent ancient forests that once covered the Northwest have been felled and their ecosystems changed forever; and an alarming number of streams and lakes are now lifeless due to pollution. And we are now discovering that even our healthiest national parks are incapable of sustaining the ecosystems indigenous to them in the long term because they are not large enough and are not surrounded by buffer zones necessary to protect them from human influence.

If we are to pass on any natural resources at all to future generations, we must stop thinking of our country and the rest of the Earth in terms of how much ore and lumber and water we can strip from them. We must begin thinking of our planet as a fragile, complex, interconnected system, sensitive to all foreign stimuli and worthy of preservation.

I am asking you to consider creating or backing legislation that: (1.) places preservation of natural resources above commercial interests in importance, especially if those resources are on federal lands; (2.) restructures federal agencies like the Forest Service in ways that enable them to look at natural resources from a wider perspective and ensure conservation rather than letting resources be plundered; and (3.) abandons expensive military programs so that more funds can be diverted toward sound, comprehensive management of natural resources.

Thank you for your consideration.

Sincerely,

—
—
—
—

—
—
—
—

RE: Stiffer fines for oil spills, toxic dumping, etc.

Dear

About 700,000 tons of toxic waste are generated in the United States every day—enough to fill the New Orleans Superdome 15,000 times a year. Some of it is spilled or illegally dumped, as are tens of thousands of other hazardous substances that are not considered wastes. Each year brings with it more horror stories like the ones from Love Canal and Three Mile Island and Prince William Sound. Every week, more oil spills contaminate our waterways, more industrial effluent pours into our streams, more radioactivity is released into our air, more gasoline leaks into our drinking water from underground tanks, more toxic chemicals are spilled on our highways, and so on.

Although the Environmental Protection Agency is supposed to cope with the problem, it cannot. It operates on a yearly budget of $8.5 billion, but it would take $30 billion to clean up just the sites that have already been identified (and ignore those that have not even been reported). Some states have their own agencies, but many of these are inadequate as well.

The problem is not that more taxes need to be appropriated, but that policy and regulations need to be rewritten. At present, EPA regulations allow generators of less than one hundred kilograms of hazardous waste per month to dispose of it as if it were ordinary garbage, without paying any fines at all. Companies whose trucks, trains, or ships are involved in accidents are often not charged for spills of oil or other hazardous substances. Industrial polluters are usually simply asked to clean up their messes. If they refuse, they may or may not be forced to comply, but only after lengthy appeals, during which many continue to pollute. Occasionally an offender is charged a fine that amounts to a slap on the wrist.

Instead, polluters should be held responsible for their actions. Offenders should immediately be enjoined from further discharges and heavily fined. If they refuse to comply, they should be jailed and charged, and their assets confiscated for payment of their fines, just as would be done had they refused to pay their income taxes. Revenues from such fines should be used to pay not only cleanup costs, but also the expense of developing alternate products that are not hazardous.

I urge you to initiate or back congressional bills designed to shift the burden of preventing and cleaning up hazardous spills and toxic-dump sites away from taxpayers and toward polluters, to place on polluters the additional burden of financing the development of alternatives that are not hazardous, and to enable the EPA and other government agencies to vigorously enforce antipollution regulations and make their charges against offenders stick.

Thank you for your consideration.

Sincerely,

—
—
—
—

—

—

—

—

RE: Economic incentives for organic farming

Dear

Every year, Americans spend huge sums of money to contaminate the
Earth with 2.7 billion pounds of pesticides in an effort to poison unwanted
insects, fungi, etc. Some fifty thousand varieties are used, most of which
have never been tested. Of those that have been tested, over one hundred of
the ingredients in them are suspected of causing cancer, birth defects, and/
or gene mutations. And many of these ingredients will be absorbed into
the food we eat and/or the water we drink. The EPA has already found
seventy-four pesticides in the groundwater of thirty-eight states in the
U.S.—the drinking water of half the American population.

Ironically, though they weaken the soil by attacking earthworms and
microorganisms that normally keep it healthy, and though they sicken and
kill birds, animals, fish, insects, and people, these pesticides lack
effectiveness. Many pests have developed an immunity to them. Over 70
types of fungi and 440 types of mites and insects are resistant to
pesticides. As a result, farmers lose about a third of their crops to pests,
just as they did before pesticides were introduced.

Meanwhile, other chemicals exacerbate the situation. Artificial chemical
fertilizers "rev up" plant growth to produce faster yields, but also
contaminate drinking water, become absorbed into foods, and cause algae
blooms that kill fish and other aquatic life in waterways. Preservatives
retard the growth of harmful bacteria, but they also retard beneficial
bacteria, and they themselves may cause cancer or other illnesses. Mixed
chemicals can result in a synergism (they can be more deleterious in
combination than they are individually).

Consequently, American food products are often not "good, wholesome food"
at all, but a chemical soup containing herbicides, fungicides, insecticides,
rodenticides, chemical fertilizers, preservatives, flavor enhancers,
emulsifiers, and so on—any one of which may be harmful to the people
who consume them.

A 1988 Louis Harris poll found that 84 percent of American adults would rather buy organic foods that do not contain these contaminants. Were they to do so, they would improve the environment and the economy as well as their own health. Aside from not eroding and wearing out soil and polluting water with pesticides and fertilizers, organic farms require less mechanization, which means less of the air pollution that causes smog, acid rain, and greenhouse warming. These farms also usually sell more of their products to local markets, so they require less transportation, which further reduces air pollution. And because weeds and bugs must be removed by hand, organic farms provide more jobs than equivalent mainstream farms.

Although organic farming is growing in popularity, it is having trouble competing because the downstream costs of normal agribusiness (the costs of health care for people dying of chemical-induced cancers, damage done to wildlife, the expense of maintaining buildings attacked by acid rain, etc.) are not included in mainstream food prices. Because of this inequity—and only because of it—organic foods (which have little or no such downstream costs, but which require more labor to produce) carry higher checkout price tags. As a result, consumers still choose mainstream items.

In light of these facts, I urge you to introduce or support federal subsidies for organic foods, funded by revenues from new taxes that force the internalization of the downstream costs of nonorganic foods. This would remove hidden subsidies that are now underwriting destructive mainstream farming.

Thank you for your consideration.

Sincerely,

—
—
—
—

RE: Use of renewable energy by the government

Dear

I believe the U.S. government should begin employing energy conservation measures and clean, renewable energy sources like solar power, wind power, and electrolytic hydrogen in each new government installation, whether it be a ship at sea, an air force base, or an office building.

The Chernobyl disaster and the insoluble problem of what to do with nuclear waste have proved that nuclear fission is too dangerous. Fossil fuels cause smog, acid rain, and global warming, and will be depleted within a few decades. Both of these alternatives threaten to virtually destroy our environment, and both require huge, centralized power generation stations to produce electricity (and/or fuel), which are easy targets for terrorist or enemy attacks. And neither provides a stable foundation for our economy.

But clean, renewable energy alternatives like photovoltaic, solar-thermal, wind, small hydroelectric, geothermal, ocean-thermal, and tide energies can never be depleted. They produce virtually no pollution. When used in conjunction with water electrolyzers, the energy produced by each of these alternative sources can be converted into hydrogen, which produces almost no pollution at all when burned, and which can be used to fuel everything from power plants to furnaces to automobiles. And they encourage decentralization, even complete energy independence—which translates into better security and a hedge against inflation.

The U.S. government already possesses all the technology it needs to begin using clean, renewable energy, but it has failed to do so except in specialized applications like satellites and remote weather stations because of simple economics. Hydrogen fuel from photovoltaic arrays would cost about two dollars for an amount equivalent to a gallon of gasoline, and electricity from most renewable sources is a bit more expensive than that from coal-fired plants. But if downstream costs of fossil fuels and nuclear fission are included in the equation (medical costs of treating people who breathe dirty air; losses of crops, fish, and buildings to acid rain and fallout; the expense of protecting Arab oil and of protecting coastal areas from ocean levels that will rise because of the greenhouse effect; etc.), renewables are already more cost-effective.

Since the government ends up paying a large percentage of these downstream costs, it actually loses money by not using more renewables (and compromises its own security, the environment, public health, and the health of the American economy at the same time). By not using more renewables, the government actually subsidizes smog, acid rain, global warming, radioactive contamination, dependence on foreign oil, the depletion of natural resources, mass migrations during oil booms, and the escalating U.S. trade deficit.

The most expeditious way to remedy this situation is to immediately begin including clean, renewable energy use in all new government designs. For instance, architects should be instructed to include solar collectors, photovoltiac modules, and wind generators in their designs for new government buildings; U.S. Navy ship designs should include solar cells and hydrogen engines; and coastal military bases should begin harnessing tide energy.

I urge you to introduce or endorse bills stipulating that agencies and offices of the U.S. government must immediately begin using clean, renewable energy alternatives in every possible application in an effort to speed up the inevitable process of phasing in clean, renewable energy and phasing out fossil fuels and nuclear power. Let's not wait until we are forced, by crises, to do so hastily.

Thank you for your consideration.

Sincerely,

—
—
—
—

—
—
—
—

RE: More use of recycled paper by the government

Dear

I believe the Congress can do the country and the environment a great service, very easily and rather painlessly, by requiring government offices to reduce the amount of paper they use, to buy more recycled paper (preferably "minimum-impact" off-white paper), and to recycle more of their wastepaper.

The United States consumes more paper than any other nation—more than 50 million tons per year. Most of this paper is made from virgin wood pulp through processes which use, for every ton of paper, 28 million Btus of energy, 24,000 gallons of water, 360 pounds of salt cake, 216 pounds of lime, 76 pounds of soda ash, and 17 trees; and produce 176 pounds of solid waste and 120 pounds of air and water pollutants (including deadly dioxin and furans). This not only depletes valuable natural resources, but also contributes to erosion, smog, acid rain, global warming, deforestation, desertification, and the extinction of plant, animal, and insect species. And because we use most paper once and discard it, paper occupies a third of our overcrowded landfill space.

All of these problems can be addressed simultaneously and forcefully by simply conserving and recycling paper. Recycling consumes no trees and up to 60 percent less water and 70 percent less energy; causes 35 percent less water pollution and up to 95 percent less air pollution; and creates five times as many jobs as virgin pulp processing. Since it is the bleaching process that generates dioxin when paper is made from virgin pulp, recycling, which requires less bleaching, creates less dioxin. And the production of minimum-impact off-white recycled paper is virtually dioxin-free.

That recycling is cost-effective is undeniable. Industries have profited from it for years, and now many municipalities and several states, awakened to the fact that recycling is the most efficient waste-management option available, have followed their lead. Maryland, for instance, has saved enough energy by recycling to heat ten thousand homes for a year.

Despite its advantages, however, recycled paper struggles to compete because of lack of consumer demand. Even though it would be cheaper if below-cost Forest Service timber sales were discontinued and downstream costs of virgin-pulp production internalized, its market price makes it appear more expensive to the consumer. Consequently, consumers are reluctant to buy it, so manufacturers are reluctant to use it—with the result that concerned citizens often collect more wastepaper than can be used, while sales of recycled products remain slow.

What is needed to break this impasse is a large demand for recycled paper, and I think the government should provide that demand. The U.S. government is by far the world's largest user of paper. The Congressional Record alone consumes a staggering amount, which is in turn dwarfed by the billions of tax forms, brochures, letters, and other documents generated by government offices. Some of these are already printed on recycled paper, but a huge number are not. I believe this is a situation that the government has an obligation to correct. I believe there is no good reason for not eventually using recycled paper in every U.S. government application from army toilet tissue to White House stationery if it will help save the world's forests and slow pollution and global warming.

While more revenue would initially be required for the procurement of recycled paper than is now budgeted, the extra outlay should more than offset over time by revenues from recycling government wastepaper, and from savings in health care payments for the effects of pollution, reforestation expenses, timber industry subsidies, support for the jobless, crop, forest, and fishery losses due to acid rain, dioxin cleanups, etc.

Thank you for your consideration.

Sincerely,

—
—
—
—

Chapter 7

Letters to Governors

Generally, the smaller a government is, the more responsive it can be to individuals' demands. Such responsiveness is fortunate, because every state, county, and municipality has laws and policies that affect the environment, and many of those policies need to be improved or even reversed.

Governors have the power to propose, validate, and veto legislation; as well as to instruct government offices; to act as liaison to other states; and to influence public opinion. Any one of these powers can determine whether a particular effort to save the Earth succeeds or fails. So it is crucial that your governor be informed of what is happening to the environment and where you stand on environmental issues. The letters in this chapter are designed to perform precisely that function.

Letter 60 is a plea for the state to adopt a beverage-container deposit law in order to keep bottles and cans out of our already overburdened landfills and to promote recycling. (If your state already has such a law, you will obviously not want to mail this letter.)

Letter 61 asks for more trees to be planted along state roads and on other state property to combat deforestation.

Letter 62 appeals to the governor to help discontinue the use of road salt.

Letter 63 asks for bans on lead shot, lead fishing weights, and lead bullets because of the damage they cause.

The rest of the letters address some of the same environmental issues dealt with in the presidential letters in chapter 5, but are phrased to promote action at the state level. A few of them may also be unnecessary in your particular case. For instance, if you live in California, you may not wish to ask for tougher emission standards.

Letter 64 concerns renewable energy alternatives.

Letter 65 asks that economic incentives be established for conservation.

Letter 66 asks the governor to support a ban on chlorofluorocarbons and halons.

Letter 67 suggests that economic incentives for recycling be established.

Letter 68 urges that tougher state emission standards be adopted.

Letter 69 proposes stiffer fines for oil spills, the dumping of toxic chemicals, and so on within the state.

Letter 70 is a plea to abandon nuclear power.

Letter 71 suggests the state government use more recycled paper.

Letter 72 asks for more use of renewable energy by the state government.

The names and addresses of the governors of each of the fifty states appear in appendix B. You can find the information about your governor by looking up your state.

The salutations of your letters should be in the following format:

Dear Governor [governor's last name]:

—
—
—
—

RE: Establishing a beverage-container deposit law

Dear Governor

I believe it's time for our state to adopt a "bottle bill" requiring deposits on beverage containers.

Trash is a serious problem all over the United States. Americans are now producing it at such a prodigious rate that the U.S. needs five undred new landfills every year. And a surprising amount of it consists of cans and bottles that could easily be recycled. Last year, Americans used enough plastic bottles to fill a four-hundred-mile-long caravan of dump trucks, enough glass bottles and jars to fill the World Trade Center's two skyscrapers twenty-six times, and enough aluminum cans to reach to the moon and back ten times. The majority of these containers were strewn along streets and highways, or buried in landfills, where they are expected to last hundreds or thousands of years.

Bottle bills have been wonderfully successful in other states. Just before New York's was introduced, the percentage of containers recycled there was 15 percent for aluminum, 4 percent for glass, and 1 percent for plastic. Three years later, the figures had changed to 60 percent for aluminum, 80 percent for glass, and 50 percent for plastic (some states with deposit laws now report that 90 percent of their containers are recycled). In just the first two years New York's law was in effect, $50 to $100 million in energy costs, $50 million in cleanup costs, and $19 million in solid waste disposal costs were saved. The recycling that bottle bills encourage creates jobs, too. New York has seen a net increase of five thousand full-time jobs (taking into account job losses in the manufacture of new containers) and Michigan has gained forty-six hundred. And emergency-room doctors in Massachusetts have even seen a 60 percent drop in cuts from glass that require stitches since that state's deposit law went into effect.

Bottle bills also lead to the preservation of vast amounts of natural resources and help to lessen air and water pollution, smog, acid rain, and global warming. For instance, every ton of aluminum that is recycled saves 8,766 pounds of bauxite, 1,020 pounds of petroleum coke, 966 pounds of soda ash, 327 pounds of pitch, 238 pounds of lime, and 177 million Btus of energy from being consumed. It also prevents 3,290 pounds of red mud, over 700 pounds of solid wastes, and 76 pounds of air pollutants from being generated.

In addition to the states mentioned above, several others have adopted the European viewpoint—that trash can be converted from a liability into an asset by recycling—and are using container deposit laws to their advantage. Oregon is the leader in recycling legislation, having passed its bottle bill nearly twenty years ago. Other pioneers include Iowa, Maine, and Vermont. I urge you to lead our state in joining them by proposing a container deposit plan to our legislature.

Thank you for your consideration.

Sincerely,

—
—
—
—

—
—
—
—

RE: Planting trees on state-owned land

Dear Governor

I am writing to ask that you propose a new program to the legislature that
will enable more trees to be planted along highways, on the grounds of
state buildings, and on other state land, and that will support volunteer
reforestation efforts.

Trees are vital to the health of the biosphere. They prevent a runaway
greenhouse effect by absorbing carbon dioxide. They stabilize soil, provide
humidification and evaporative cooling (as much as ten degrees in urban
areas), and emit the major portion of the oxygen we breathe. They also
provide food, wood, shade, and beauty for us, and shelter many of the
Earth's plant, animal, and insect species.

Unfortunately, we have been cutting trees down at an escalating rate for so
many centuries that we now stand on the brink of environmental
catastrophe. We are razing the 70-million-year-old tropical rain forests
that produce 40 percent of the oxygen in the air at the rate of 51 acres per
minute. If this continues, they may all be gone by the year 2032. About
87 percent of the original ancient forests in the northwestern U.S. are
already gone. Canada cuts 247,000 more acres of trees than it replants
every year. And all over the world, trees are constantly being bulldozed for
farms, buildings, highways, and parking lots, and never replaced.

This deforestation is one of the reasons carbon dioxide, which traps solar
heat and creates a greenhouse effect, has reached such a high
concentration in our atmosphere that global warming has begun. Global
average temperatures are already about half a degree higher than a century
ago, and they could rise by as much as nine degrees in the next few
decades. This would melt the Earth's ice caps, flood coastal areas, turn
farmland into desert, and spawn frequent, violent storms.

This greenhouse effect is progressive. Even if we stop burning gasoline and coal to prevent more carbon dioxide from building up in the air, global warming will continue for years unless we do something to remove the carbon dioxide already in the air—something as simple as planting more trees.

If we were able to grow enough trees, we could stabilize our atmosphere and bring global warming to a halt, buying ourselves some time to develop alternate fuels. Of course, a project of that magnitude is beyond the ability of any one state or even any one nation. But every tree planted, regardless of its location, helps reduce the level of carbon dioxide in the air a little bit, thereby slowing the greenhouse effect.

Grassroots tree-planting projects have already begun all over the world. The American Forestry Association's Global Releaf program, for instance, which began on Arbor Day, 1989, is helping Americans plant 100 million trees by 1992. But more government involvement is needed. Every state and every county needs to pitch in and do its share by including more trees in government building projects, by aiding volunteer efforts at reforestation and education, by publicly endorsing tree planting, and by passing legislation sponsoring tree plantings by individual volunteers and organizations like the Boy Scouts of America.

Please join those of us who support reforestation by announcing your endorsement, and by proposing a plan to the legislature to provide seedlings and guidelines for anyone wishing to plant trees on state property.

Thank you for your consideration.

Sincerely,

—
—
—
—

—
—
—
—

RE: Discontinuing the salting of roads and bridges

Dear Governor

It seems to me our environment is beleaguered enough by contamination
from leaking landfills, automobile exhaust, agricultural chemicals, and
industrial wastes. Why must we spread tons of another harmful substance
around it nearly every time it snows?

Road salt is destructive. It kills most species of plants, retards the growth
of fish eggs and fry in lakes, and retards the mixing of upper and lower
layers of lake water that promotes the growth of bottom-dwelling
invertebrates. It eats away car bodies, deteriorates road surfaces, corrodes
bridges, and attacks underground cables and pipelines. It even taints
groundwater, as many Massachusetts residents discovered when they had
to close down nine municipal wells and one hundred private wells because
of road-salt contamination. And once the cost of all this damage is factored
into the price of road salt, the $25 per ton most street departments pay
increases 6,400 percent to a whopping $1,600 per ton!

Clearly, alternatives are needed. And many exist. Some communities use
dark cinders, which increase traction and aid melting by absorbing
sunlight. Others are trying a special paving material that inhibits icing.
In some mountainous areas where constant snowplowing renders additives
useless, snow-tire/chain laws and driver education work well to keep traffic
flowing.

I want you to know that I support the abandonment of salting as a means
of clearing snowy roadways in our state, even if no alternative method of
clearing is adopted.

Thank you for your consideration.

Sincerely,

—
—
—
—

—
—
—
—

RE: Banning lead shot, bullets, and fishing weights

Dear Governor

Many experts identify lead as the leading toxic-substance problem in the country today. According to EPA estimates, the drinking water of 10 million American children and 32 million adults is contaminated with dangerous amounts of lead.

Lead concentrates in soft tissues, blood, and bones. Tiny amounts of it can cause changes in behavior and sleep patterns, irritability, loss of appetite, and fatigue. Larger amounts can cause fainting, vomiting, convulsions, coma, impairment of the digestive system, neurological disorders, high blood pressure, kidney damage, and damage to child brain development.

Lead water pipes, lead-based paints, and leaded gasoline are being phased out because of the health risk they pose. But lead shot and bullets used by hunters and lead weights used in fishing still enjoy widespread use, even though they are similarly dangerous. Waterfowl eat them, then die excruciating deaths seventeen to twenty-one days later because of the paralysis of their digestive tracts. Fish also become poisoned when they swallow them. Predators that eat affected birds and fish—including human beings—are poisoned in turn. And the lead that is not eaten contaminates ponds, lakes, streams, rivers, and groundwater by slowly dissolving, especially in areas where acid rain falls.

Shot, bullets, and sinkers need not be made of lead. Some states already require shot to be made of steel, and steel sinkers are now being used in England. I urge you to work toward banning lead shot, bullets, and sinkers in our state, and toward educating our citizens about the dangers of lead poisoning. And I hope you will make use of every opportunity to encourage the governors of other states to do the same.

Thank you for your consideration.

Sincerely,

—
—
—

—
—
—
—

RE: Supporting renewable energy alternatives

Dear Governor

I urge you to take steps to develop the vast potential of clean, renewable energy available in our state.

As the Gulf War clearly demonstrated, oil is a finite commodity that is becoming more precious each day. It is estimated that unless oil usage slows, the world's oil will be depleted during the next century. Unfortunately, oil usage is expanding instead. We are using more in the U.S., and developing nations are rushing to emulate us. This is bound to cause prices to spiral higher until all the oil is gone.

Meanwhile, oil poisons us and destroys our planet. In the U.S., cars emit 20 percent of the fossil-fuel carbon dioxide that contributes to global warming; 34 percent of the nitrogen oxide that kills crops, lakes, and forests when it turns into acid rain; and 27 percent of the hydrocarbons that ruin our lungs with ozone smog. Diesels, home heating, and smokestack exhaust from utilities and oil and chemical plants produce even greater amounts. And every year thousands of oil and gasoline spills make life impossible in waterways, pollute drinking water, and cost billions of dollars in cleanups and fire losses.

Coal is an even worse air polluter than oil. And nuclear power is dying because spent nuclear fuel that stays radioactive for fifty thousand years cannot be disposed of safely, and because even the billions spent to build "fail-safe" backup systems cannot prevent catastrophic accidents. Also, oil, coal, and nuclear fires all promote global warming by adding to the total amount of heat in the atmosphere.

But clean, renewable energy alternatives like photovoltaic, solar-thermal, wind, small hydroelectric, geothermal, ocean-thermal, and tide energies can combat all these problems simultaneously. Each is virtually pollution-free compared with fossil fuels. When used in conjunction with water electrolyzers, the energy produced by each of these alternative sources can be converted into hydrogen, which produces almost no pollution at all when burned, and which can fuel everything from power plants to furnaces to automobiles. And none of them artificially adds heat to the atmosphere.

Renewables also afford the added benefit of strengthening our state's economy. By encouraging decentralization of energy production, they bolster competition and create more local jobs, smoothing out the boom/bust cycle that oil fosters. They can free us from the need to buy fuel or energy from other states or countries, and from price spirals caused by increasing demands for oil. And any excess energy they produce can be exported.

All the technology needed to greatly expand the use of clean renewables is available, but it remains idle because of simple economics. Hydrogen fuel from photovoltaic arrays would cost about two dollars for an amount equivalent to a gallon of gasoline, and electricity from most renewable sources is a bit more expensive than that from coal-fired plants. But if downstream costs of fossil fuels and fission are included in the equation (medical costs of treating people who breathe dirty air; losses of crops, fish, and buildings to acid rain and fallout; the expense of protecting coastal areas from ocean levels that will rise because of the greenhouse effect; etc.), then renewables are already cheaper.

In light of these conditions, I urge you to give renewable energy companies incentives to locate in our state, to ask the legislature to provide increased funding for renewable energy development in our state and tax advantages for residents who buy renewable alternatives, and to push for the mandatory internalization of the downstream costs of fossil fuels and nuclear power. And I encourage you to share these ideas with federal officials and the governors of the other states.

Thank you for your consideration.

Sincerely,

—
—
—
—

—

—

—

—

<u>RE</u>: Establishing economic incentives for conservation

Dear Governor

The oil embargo of the 1970s triggered a number of energy conservation measures in the United States. One was the establishment of federal income tax "energy credits," which have since expired. I believe the tax credit idea was a good one. Because of it, a lot of Americans insulated their homes, invested in solar collectors, etc., and helped to ameliorate the "energy crisis" the country was wrestling with at that time.

Now we face a much more severe crisis. Even before Saddam Hussein threw the world's oil-based economy into turmoil, the U.S. trade deficit had grown to gigantic proportions, largely because we import nearly half the oil we use. But the consequences of that deficit, enormous though they may be, pale in comparison to two other energy problems that face us today. One is pollution. Smog, acid rain, and global warming—all largely attributable to energy use—are rapidly destroying our environment. Many experts agree that they have reached crisis stage around the world. The other problem is oil depletion. The world's oil supply is projected to be virtually used up during the next century.

Climatologists, ecologists, and economists agree that energy conservation is one of our most potent weapons against these problems. I believe our state should do its part to encourage conservation by instituting tax breaks favoring manufacturers of energy-saving devices and residents who add insulation, storm windows, high-efficiency furnaces, etc. to their existing homes and businesses, and by restructuring vehicle licensing fees to make them inversely proportional to mileage rates.

Of course, conservation in one state cannot solve the global environmental and energy crises. Before that can be accomplished, clean, renewable energy sources must also be developed, and deforestation must be stopped and reforestation begun around the world. But I believe measures like those I have suggested above must be adopted if we are to avert economic and environmental disaster, and I would be proud to see our state become a leader in adopting them. I urge you to propose such incentives to the legislature, and to encourage the governors of other states to consider following similar paths.

Thank you for your consideration.

Sincerely,

—
—
—
—

—
—
—
—

RE: Banning chlorofluorocarbons and halons

Dear Governor

Even as law enforcement agencies make every effort to keep illegal drugs out of our state, chemicals that may ultimately be even more destructive are being used legally. I refer to chlorofluorocarbons (or CFCs) and halons.

Scientists have now determined beyond all doubt that these chemicals are responsible for the destruction of the Earth's protective ozone layer. Studies show that as much as 6.2 percent of it is already gone, and the rate of deterioration is accelerating because the amount of CFCs and halons in the air is increasing and each molecule of them can destroy up to ten thousand molecules of ozone in the upper atmosphere.

As more of this protective layer disappears, more ultraviolet solar radiation will leak through to the Earth's surface, damaging living things, including human beings. Popular accounts have focused on the few thousand additional cases of skin cancer we are likely to see as a short-term consequence, but the problem is much more grave than that. There will probably be increases in cataracts and other signs of premature aging in humans and other animals; damage to immune systems; reductions in crop, timber, fish, and ranch yields; an upset of the fragile marine ecology; decreases in the size of plant foliage; and eventually a general decline, perhaps a total collapse, of the Earth's entire biosphere.

As if that were not enough, the same chemicals are also responsible for up to 20 percent of the greenhouse effect because they trap up to twenty thousand times as much solar heat as does an equal amount of carbon dioxide. And as greater volumes of them are released, that percentage— and the subsequent rate of global warming—will grow dramatically. So, even if efforts to replace fossil fuels with clean energy sources succeed, we still may soon face rising sea levels and an increase in the frequency and severity of storms unless we stop the emission of these substances.

Of course, the federal government showed its recognition of the problem years ago when it banned the use of CFCs as aerosol propellants throughout the U.S. But since that time their use in other applications has multiplied. And while some manufacturers and users have admitted the dangers and voluntarily opted to quit buying and selling them, many have not. The electronics industry employs them extensively as solvents. Hospitals use them as sterilants. Polystyrene and other plastic foams are full of them. Nearly every family in America now owns a refrigerator and/or air conditioner that uses them. And almost every CFC molecule will eventually seep into the air. Halons are less ubiquitous, but are used in fire extinguishers, and so are released not accidentally, but by design.

More benign substitutes for CFCs and halons have been identified for virtually every application. They are now less convenient and/or more costly, but they are necessary—the price of not switching to them is unconscionable. Some plans have already been made to phase these alternatives in, but I believe these plans are too little too late. The situation is much too serious to allow the possible economic consequences to any particular business to get in the way of immediately substituting safer chemicals.

To help solve this potentially devastating problem, I urge you to work with the legislature and the various state agencies to ban, statewide, the manufacture and distribution of CFCs and halons, to impose new import restrictions that prevent them from entering the borders of our state, and to encourage the development of safer alternatives through economic incentives such as income tax breaks for manufacturers and consumers of such alternatives. And I ask that you try to influence other governors to join you in your effort.

Thank you for your consideration.

Sincerely,

—
—
—
—

—
—
—
—

RE: Establishing economic incentives for recycling

Dear Governor

Like many residents of our state, I have grown very concerned about the
environment. I believe that because we Americans cause more smog, acid
rain, and greenhouse warming than anybody else, we should be doing more
to combat those problems—not just for our own benefit, but for the benefit
of our children and succeeding generations as well. And I know of no
better way to begin than to do more to promote the recycling of paper right
here in our state.

Every year, 850 million trees are cut to make the 50 million tons of paper
Americans use. Much of it comes from the disappearing rain forests that
until recently have harbored half the world's plant and animal species and
helped prevent a runaway greenhouse effect by absorbing carbon dioxide
and producing 40 percent of the oxygen in our atmosphere. A lot of it
comes from timber cut from our own federal lands. Virtually all of it ends
up in our landfills, exacerbating the problem cities face as they run out of
room to dispose of solid wastes. Worse, the paper industry contributes
greatly to smog, acid rain, and global warming because it is the largest
single industrial user of fuel oil. And its processes use billions of gallons
of our diminishing supplies of clean water and create large amounts of
deadly dioxin.

Every ton of recycled paper saves 17 trees, 7,000 gallons of water, and the
equivalent of 4,100 kilowatt-hours of electricity or 380 gallons of oil—
enough to heat the average home for six months. It also causes 35 percent
less water pollution and up to 95 percent less air pollution, and keeps open
as much landfill area as an "average" resident of our state uses in a year.
And recycling creates jobs—five times as many people are needed to
produce a ton of recycled paper as are needed to put out the same amount
of product using virgin wood pulp (and the workers need not be located
near forests).

However, because of the U.S. Forest Service's policy of selling timber below cost (which indirectly subsidizes virgin pulp production and discourages recycling), and because timber and pulp industries aren't required to include downstream costs in prices for logs and virgin pulp, recycled paper is having a hard time competing. Consumers are hesitant to buy recycled paper products because they are more expensive, so manufacturers are reluctant to use recycled paper. As a result, discarded newspapers sit waiting for buyers while the recycled paper industry struggles to grow.

Together we can help to right this situation. I urge you to take action to help save our environment by proposing to our legislature a plan for new state statutes that will tax products made from virgin wood pulp in order to provide tax credits for recycled products. And I ask that you challenge other governors to propose similar plans in their own states.

Thank you for your consideration.

Sincerely,

—
—
—
—

—

—

—

—

RE: Adopting tough state emission standards

Dear Governor

In my opinion, our state needs to adopt stringent air pollution standards.
The exhausts from every vehicle and smokestack within its borders
contribute to the world's growing air pollution problems, and those
problems have reached crisis stage. Smog and acid rain are destroying
forests, fisheries, and crops around the world. According to the EPA, over
76 million Americans are breathing air that does not meet the clean-air
standards. And it is now clear that global warming is not a fanciful idea,
but a harsh reality.

Vehicles are a large part of the problem. According to the Department of
Transportation, every year an average car in the U.S. logs over ten thousand
miles, burns over five hundred gallons of gasoline, and pumps over ten
thousand pounds of carbon dioxide into the air. Cars emit 20 percent of
the fossil-fuel carbon dioxide, 27 percent of the hydrocarbons, and 34
percent of the nitrogen oxides that go into the air in the U.S. Trucks and
buses are even worse polluters than cars.

Chemical and oil plants and utilities are the sources of about half our
nitrogen oxide and hydrocarbon pollutants. They also produce huge
amounts of carbon dioxide, as well as particulates, sulfur dioxide, and other
harmful gases.

That these emissions must be reduced before smog, acid rain, and global
warming can be brought into check is without question. But federal efforts
to do so have historically been tardy and unfocused. The U.S. is still widely
regarded as the world's most wasteful nation and its worst polluter.
During the 1980s, clean-air regulations that were inadequate to begin with
were relaxed or disregarded time after time as federal officials bowed to the
lobbying efforts of oil, chemical, and automobile companies. Washington
placed the profitability of those companies above the health of the
environment and the American public. And the federal clean-air
legislation introduced in 1990 was too little too late to solve the problem.

But we can insist on clean air in our state. We can begin by adopting tough emission laws like those the state of California has pioneered. We can continue by studying Japan, which now has the strictest limits on emissions of any country, and by funneling the revenues received from penalties into the development of clean, renewable energy sources that will ultimately reduce emissions. And we can finish the job by sticking to our commitment, by enforcing the law, and by levying heavy fines against polluters and then collecting those fines—even forcing offenders out of business if necessary—rather than relaxing requirements to cater to special interests.

I hope you will take these steps to protect the inalienable right of every resident of this state—and of every living thing on this planet—to breathe clean air; and to join other states that have begun the fight against the ravages of air pollution. And I hope you will make use of every opportunity to encourage other governors to act similarly in their own states.

Thank you for your consideration.

Sincerely,

—
—
—
—

—
—
—
—

RE: Stiffer fines for oil spills, toxic dumping, etc.

Dear Governor

Each year brings with it more horror stories like the ones from Love Canal
and Three Mile Island and Prince William Sound. Every week, more oil
spills contaminate the Earth's waterways, more industrial effluent pours
into our streams, more radioactivity is released into our air, more gasoline
leaks into our drinking water from underground tanks, more toxic
chemicals are spilled on our highways, and so on.

Although the U.S. Environmental Protection Agency is supposed to cope
with the problem, it cannot. It operates on a yearly budget of $8.5 billion,
but it would take $30 billion to clean up just the sites that have already
been identified (and ignore those that have not even been reported).

So the EPA compromises. It allows generators of less than one hundred
kilograms of hazardous waste per month to dispose of it as if it were
ordinary garbage, without paying any fines at all. Companies whose
trucks, trains, or ships are involved in accidents are often not charged for
spills of oil or other hazardous substances. Industrial polluters are usually
simply asked to clean up their messes. If they refuse, they may or may not
be prosecuted. If judges rule against them, they may or may not be forced
to comply, but only after lengthy appeals, during which many continue to
pollute. Occasionally an offender is charged a fine that amounts to a slap
on the wrist.

Instead, polluters should be held responsible for their actions. Offenders
should immediately be enjoined from further discharges and heavily fined.
If they refuse to comply, they should be jailed and charged, and their assets
seized for payment of their fines, just as would happen if they refused to
pay their income taxes. Revenues from such fines should be used to pay
not only cleanup costs, but also the expense of developing alternative
products that are not hazardous.

What I ask of you is that you work with the EPA, the legislature, and the state agencies involved to develop state policies and statutes that fill the gap between what the EPA and our state are doing now and what needs to be done. What we need are policies and laws that shift the burden of preventing and cleaning up hazardous spills and toxic dump sites away from taxpayers and toward polluters, and that place on polluters the additional burden of financing the development of alternatives that are not hazardous. And I ask that you encourage other governors to follow your lead.

Thank you for your consideration.

Sincerely,

—
—
—
—

—
—
—
—

RE: Abandoning nuclear power

Dear Governor

Decades ago, when we decided to split atoms to meet the tremendous electricity demands of the future, we made two assumptions that were gravely in error. We assumed that nuclear accidents could be prevented and that science would soon find a safe way to dispose of nuclear wastes.

Nuclear accidents cannot be prevented, regardless of how many billions of dollars are spent on "fail-safe" backup systems. Nuclear Regulatory Commission documents show that more than thirty-three thousand mishaps, one thousand of which are considered significant, have occurred in U.S. power plants since the Three Mile Island incident in 1979. Testifying before the Energy and Power Subcommittee of the House Committee on Energy and Commerce in 1986, NRC Commissioner James Asseltine suggested a serious accident is likely in the U.S. within two decades. The probability of a major core-melt during that period has been put at 45 percent by an NRC projection.

Such an accident would be catastrophic. The Chernobyl accident in 1986 displaced 135,000 people from 179 villages; killed 31 people outright; irradiated so many that tens of thousands of cancer deaths, birth defects, and genetic mutations are expected; contaminated huge amounts of crops, livestock, and wildlife in several countries; and cost the Soviets $13 billion (including the loss of the power plant). An Atomic Energy Commission study done years ago estimated that a meltdown in the U.S. could injure 73,000 and kill 27,000, while causing $17 billion in property damage.

The so-called "inherently safe" reactors that have been proposed may be feasible to build decades from now, but even they are untenable, because we will still have no means of safely disposing of the spent fuel they generate.

Such waste already presents serious problems. Since it stays dangerously radioactive for fifty thousand years and cannot be safely disposed of, voters who don't want it near them defeat dump site proposals. As a result, it is only temporarily stored. By the year 2001, we may have seventy-two thousand tons of it. And by that time we will also have enough low-level milling and mining waste to build a mound as high as a man's head from New York to Los Angeles.

If waste from fission reactors is dangerous, building the nuclear weapons they make possible is insane. As Carl Sagan and others have pointed out, a nuclear conflict cannot be won, because in addition to releasing deadly radiation, it would result in a "nuclear winter." According to the DOE, U.S. laboratories and plants that make nuclear weapons have released radioactive isotopes on at least 155 occasions (no one knows how many instances may have gone unreported). This pollution has probably caused thousands of cancers and birth defects in humans and an incalculable amount of damage to wildlife, and Congress has estimated that it will cost up to $200 billion over the next hundred years to clean it up. Nuclear weapons testing is credited with even greater damage. According to Dr. John Gofman, atomic testing has probably already condemned 1,116,000 people to developing lung cancer. Ironically, our nuclear weapons may already be obsolete; the threat of Soviet aggression, which they were designed to deter, seems to have disintegrated.

I am opposed to the exorbitant rates for electricity that nuclear plants charge. I resent being contaminated. And I am sick of worrying that some human error or some software or hardware glitch might trigger a world-ending launch of nuclear warheads that nobody wants. Please join me in my effort to see nuclear waste repositories and nuclear power in any form outlawed in our state, and please encourage the governors of other states to work for similar results in their states.

Thank you for your consideration.

Sincerely,

—
—
—
—

_____, 199_

_

—
—
—
—

RE: More use of recycled paper by the government

Dear Governor

I believe your office and the other state offices can do the environment a great service, very easily and rather painlessly, by simply reducing the amount of paper they use, buying more recycled paper (preferably "minimum-impact" off-white paper), and recycling more of their waste-paper.

Most paper is made from virgin wood pulp by processes which use, for every ton of paper, 28 million Btus of energy, 24,000 gallons of water, 360 pounds of salt cake, 216 pounds of lime, 76 pounds of soda ash, and 17 trees, and produce 176 pounds of solid waste and 120 pounds of air and water pollutants (including deadly dioxin and furans). This not only depletes valuable natural resources, but also contributes to erosion, smog, acid rain, global warming, deforestation, desertification, and the extinction of plant, animal, and insect species. And because we use most paper once and discard it, paper occupies a third of our overcrowded landfill space.

All of these problems can be combated simultaneously and forcefully by simply conserving and recycling paper. Recycling consumes no trees and up to 60 percent less water and 70 percent less energy, causes 35 percent less water pollution and up to 95 percent less air pollution and creates five times as many jobs as virgin pulp processing. Since it is the bleaching process that generates dioxin when paper is made from virgin pulp, recycling, which requires less bleaching, creates less dioxin. And the production of minimum-impact off-white recycled paper is virtually dioxin-free.

That recycling is cost-effective is undeniable. Industries have profited from it for years, and now many municipalities and several states, awakened to the fact that recycling is the most efficient waste-management option available, have followed their lead. Maryland, for instance, has saved enough energy by recycling to heat ten thousand homes for a year.

Despite its advantages, though, recycled paper struggles to compete because of lack of consumer demand. Even though it would be cheaper if below-cost Forest Service timber sales were discontinued and downstream costs of virgin-pulp pollution internalized, its market price makes it appear more expensive to the consumer. Consequently, consumers are reluctant to buy it, so manufacturers hesitate to use it—with the result that concerned citizens often collect more wastepaper than can be used, while sales of recycled products remain slow.

What is needed to break this impasse is a large demand for recycled paper, and I think our state government should help provide that demand by printing more of the thousands of tax forms, brochures, letters, and other documents generated by state offices on recycled paper and by using recycled paper in other areas. I see no good reason for not eventually using it in every state application from highway department toilet tissue to supreme court documents if it will help save the world's forests and slow pollution and global warming.

I urge you to work with the legislature and the various state agencies to increase the government's use of recycled paper, and to encourage the governors of other states to do the same.

Thank you for your consideration.

Sincerely,

—
—
—
—

—
—
—
—

RE: Use of renewable energy by the government

Dear Governor

I believe our state should begin employing more energy conservation measures and more clean, renewable, alternative energy sources like solar power, wind power, and electrolytic hydrogen in each new government installation, whether it be a new prison building, new highway lighting, or the remodeling of a university.

The Chernobyl disaster and the insoluble problem of what to do with nuclear wastes have proved that nuclear fission is too dangerous. Fossil fuels cause smog, acid rain, and global warming and will be depleted within a few decades. Both threaten to virtually destroy our environment, and both require huge, centralized power generation stations to produce electricity (and/or fuel), which are easy targets for terrorists. And neither provides a stable foundation for our economy.

But clean, renewable energy alternatives like photovoltaic, solar-thermal, wind, small hydroelectric, geothermal, ocean-thermal, and tide energies can never be depleted. They produce virtually no pollution. When used in conjunction with water electrolyzers, the energy produced by each of them can be converted into hydrogen, which produces almost no pollution at all when burned, and which can be used to fuel everything from power plants to furnaces to automobiles. And they encourage decentralization, even complete energy independence—which translates into better security and a hedge against inflation.

We already possess all the technology needed to begin using more clean, renewable energy, but we have failed to do so because of simple economics. Hydrogen fuel from photovoltaic arrays would cost about two dollars for an amount equivalent to a gallon of gasoline, and electricity from most renewable sources is a bit more expensive than that from coal-fired plants. But if downstream costs of fossil fuels and nuclear fission are included in the equation (medical costs of treating people who breathe dirty air; losses of crops, fish, and buildings to acid rain and fallout; storm damage resulting from global warming; etc.), renewables are already more cost-effective.

Since governments end up paying a large percentage of these downstream costs, and since they are concerned with long-term rather than short-term investments, they actually lose money by not using more renewables (and compromise their own security, the environment, and public health at the same time). By not using more renewables, governments in effect subsidize smog, acid rain, global warming, radioactive contamination, dependence on foreign oil, the depletion of natural resources, dislocation of populations during oil booms, and escalating trade deficits.

The most expeditious way to remedy this situation is to immediately begin including conservation and clean, renewable energy use in all new government designs. For instance, architects should be instructed to include solar collectors, photovoltaic modules, and wind generators in their designs for new state buildings and remodeling projects. Highway engineers should call for solar lighting at illuminated intersections. State offices should coordinate car pools for their employees. And so on.

I urge you to endorse more use of energy conservation measures and the use of more clean, renewable energy alternatives in every possible application in our state. Let's speed up the inevitable process of phasing in clean, renewable energy and phasing out fossil fuels and nuclear power, instead of waiting until we are forced, by crises, to do so hastily.

Thank you for your consideration.

Sincerely,

—
—
—
—

Chapter 8

Letters to State Legislators

This chapter contains letters aimed at the people who represent you in your state legislature. They closely resemble the gubernatorial letters for the same reasons the congressional letters in chapter 6 parallel the presidential letters in chapter 5.

Letter 73 concerns drink-container deposit laws.

Letter 74 concerns planting more trees on state land.

Letter 75 asks that roads not be salted.

Letter 76 requests bans on lead shot, bullets, etc.

Letter 77 asks for support of energy alternatives.

Letter 78 concerns incentives for conservation.

Letter 79 suggests banning CFCs and halons.

Letter 80 concerns economic incentives for recycling.

Letter 81 is a plea for tougher emission standards.

Letter 82 asks for stiffer fines for oil spills, etc.

Letter 83 urges the abandonment of nuclear power.

Letter 84 urges that the state use recycled paper.

Letter 85 concerns state use of renewable energy.

As is the case with the gubernatorial letters in the previous chapter, you should read these letters carefully to determine whether or not they apply in the case of your particular state. If, for instance, your state has already been declared a "nuclear-free zone," requests for a ban on nuclear power might only make your legislator less efficient by clogging his or her mailbox.

A list of state legislators would be too long to include here. To obtain the names and addresses of those who represent you, check with the reference librarian at your library, call your county courthouse or city hall, or contact the legislature itself. This information may also be available from your local newspaper office, a voter organization, political action committee, or even a Welcome Wagon representative.

Be sure to use the proper title (The Honorable John Smith:) and an appropriate greeting (Dear Senator Smith:).

You will probably wish to send these letters to more than one recipient. Before making copies, be sure to read the special provisions on the copyright page of this book.

—

—

—

—

RE: Establishing a beverage-container deposit law

Dear

I urge you to introduce or support legislation requiring deposits on beverage containers in our state—a so-called "bottle bill."

Trash is a serious problem all over the United States. Americans are now producing it at such a prodigious rate that the U.S. needs five hundred new landfills every year. And a surprising amount of it consists of cans and bottles that could easily be recycled. This year we will discard 115 billion beer and soft-drink cans and bottles. If we were to lay these empty containers end to end, they would circle the Earth more than 435 times. The majority of them will be strewn along streets and highways, or buried in landfills, where some are expected to last hundreds or thousands of years.

Bottle bills have been wonderfully successful in other states. Just before New York's was introduced, the percentage of containers recycled there was 15 percent for aluminum, 4 percent for glass, and 1 percent for plastic. Three years later, the figures had changed to 60 percent for aluminum, 80 percent for glass, and 50 percent for plastic (some states with deposit laws now report that 90 percent of their containers are recycled). In just the first two years New York's law was in effect, $50 to $100 million in energy costs, $50 million in cleanup costs, and $19 million in solid waste disposal costs were saved. The recycling that bottle bills encourage creates jobs, too. New York has seen a net increase of five thousand full-time jobs (taking into account job losses in the manufacture of new containers) and Michigan has gained forty-six hundred. And emergency room doctors in Massachusetts have even seen a 60 percent drop in cuts from glass that require stitches since that state's deposit law went into effect.

Bottle bills also lead to the preservation of vast amounts of natural resources and help to lessen air and water pollution, smog, acid rain, and global warming. For instance, every ton of aluminum that is recycled saves 8,766 pounds of bauxite, 1,020 pounds of petroleum coke, 966 pounds of soda ash, 327 pounds of pitch, 238 pounds of lime, and 177 million Btus of energy from being consumed, and it also prevents 3,290 pounds of red mud, over 700 pounds of solid wastes, and 76 pounds of air pollutants from being generated.

In addition to the states mentioned above, several others have adopted the European viewpoint—that trash can be converted from a liability into an asset by recycling—and are using container deposit laws to their advantage. Oregon is the leader in recycling legislation, having passed its bottle bill nearly twenty years ago. Other pioneers include Iowa, Maine, and Vermont. Please help our state join them.

Thank you for your consideration.

Sincerely,

—
—
—
—

—
—
—
—

RE: Planting trees on state-owned land

Dear

I am writing to ask that you introduce or back legislation that will enable more trees to be planted along highways, on the grounds of state buildings, and on other state land; and that will support volunteer reforestation efforts.

Trees are vital to the health of the biosphere. They prevent a runaway greenhouse effect by absorbing carbon dioxide, stabilizing soil, providing humidification and evaporative cooling (as much as ten degrees in urban areas), and emitting the major portion of the oxygen we breathe. They also provide food, wood, shade, and beauty for us; and shelter the majority of the Earth's plant, animal, and insect species.

Unfortunately, we have been cutting trees down at an escalating rate for so many centuries that we now stand on the brink of environmental catastrophe. We are razing the 70 million-year-old tropical rain forests that produce 40 percent of the oxygen in the air at the rate of 51 acres per minute. At this rate they may all be gone by the year 2032. About 87 percent of the original ancient forests in the northwestern U.S. is already gone. Canada cuts 247,000 more acres of trees than it replants every year. And all over the world, trees are constantly being bulldozed for farms, buildings, highways, and parking lots, and never replaced.

This deforestation is one of the reasons carbon dioxide, which traps solar heat and creates a greenhouse effect, has reached such a high concentration in our atmosphere that global warming has begun. Average global temperatures are already about half a degree higher than a century ago, and they could rise by as much as nine degrees in the next few decades, melting the Earth's ice caps, flooding coastal areas, turning farmland into desert, and spawning frequent, violent storms.

This greenhouse effect is progressive. Even if we stop burning gasoline and coal to prevent more carbon dioxide from building up in the atmosphere, global warming will continue for years unless we do something to remove the carbon dioxide already in the air—something as simple as planting more trees.

Were we able to grow enough trees, we could stabilize our atmosphere and bring global warming to a halt, buying ourselves some time to develop alternative fuels. Of course a project of that magnitude is beyond the ability of any one state or even any nation. But every tree planted, regardless of its location, helps reduce the level of carbon dioxide in the air a little bit, thereby slowing the greenhouse effect.

Grassroots tree-planting projects have already begun all over the world. The American Forestry Association's Global Relief program, for instance, which began on Arbor Day, 1989, is helping Americans plant 100 million trees by 1992. But more government involvement is needed. Every state and every country needs to pitch in and do its share by including more trees in government building projects, by aiding volunteer efforts at reforestation and education, by publicly endorsing tree planting, and by passing legislation sponsoring tree plantings by individual volunteers and organizations like the Boy Scouts of America.

Please join those of us who support reforestation by announcing your endorsement, and by voting for bills to provide seedlings and guidelines for anyone wishing to plant trees on state property.

Thank you for your consideration.

Sincerely,

—
—
—
—

—
—
—
—

RE: Discontinuing the salting of roads and bridges

Dear

It seems to me that our environment is beleaguered enough by contamination from leaking landfills, automobile exhaust, agricultural chemicals, and industrial wastes. Why must we spread tons of another harmful substance around it nearly every time it snows?

Road salt is destructive. It kills most species of plants, retards the growth of fish eggs and fry in lakes, and retards the mixing of upper and lower layers of lake water that promotes the growth of bottom-dwelling invertebrates. It eats away car bodies, deteriorates road surfaces, corrodes bridges, and attacks underground cables and pipelines. It even taints groundwater, as many Massachusetts residents discovered when they had to close down nine municipal wells and one hundred private wells because of road-salt contamination. And once the cost of all this damage is factored into the price of road salt, the $25 per ton most street departments pay increases 6,400 percent to a whopping $1,600 per ton!

Clearly, alternatives are needed. And many exist. Some communities use dark cinders, which increase traction and aid melting by absorbing sunlight. Others are trying a special paving material that inhibits icing. In some mountainous areas where constant snowplowing renders additives useless, snow-tire/chain laws and driver education work well to keep traffic flowing.

I want you to know that I support the abandonment of salting as a means of clearing snowy roadways in our state, even if no alternative method of clearing is adopted.

Thank you for your consideration.

Sincerely,

—
—
—
—

—
—
—
—

RE: Banning lead shot, bullets, and fishing weights

Dear

I believe our state needs a statute that bans the use of lead for ammunition and fishing tackle, and that alerts the public to the dangers of lead poisoning.

Many experts identify lead as the leading toxic-substance problem in the country today. According to EPA estimates, the drinking water of 10 million American children and 32 million adults is contaminated with dangerous amounts of it.

Lead concentrates in soft tissues, blood, and bones. Tiny amounts of it can cause irritability, loss of appetite, fatigue, and changes in behavior and sleep patterns. Larger amounts can cause fainting, vomiting, convulsions, coma, impairment of the digestive system, neurological disorders, high blood pressure, kidney damage, and damage to child brain development.

Lead water pipes, lead-based paints, and leaded gasoline are being phased out because of the health risks they pose. But lead shot and bullets used by hunters and lead weights used in fishing still enjoy widespread use, even though they are similarly dangerous. Waterfowl eat them, then die excruciating deaths seventeen to twenty-one days later because of the paralysis of their digestive tracts. Fish also become poisoned when they swallow them. Predators that eat poisoned birds and fish—including human beings—get poisoned in turn. And the lead that is not eaten contaminates ponds, lakes, streams, rivers, and groundwater by slowly dissolving, especially in areas where acid rain falls.

Ammunition and "sinkers" need not be made of lead. Some states already require shot to be made of steel, and steel sinkers are now being used in

England. I urge you to work for the passage of legislation that bans lead shot, bullets, and sinkers in our state, and that helps educate our citizens about the dangers of lead poisoning.

Thank you for your consideration.

Sincerely,

—
—
—
—

—
—
—
—

RE: Supporting renewable energy alternatives

Dear

I urge you to author or back legislation designed to develop the vast potential of clean, renewable energy available in our state.

The Gulf War made it clear that oil is a finite commodity that is becoming more precious each day. It is estimated that unless oil usage slows, the world's oil supply will be depleted during the next century. Unfortunately, usage is expanding instead. We are using more oil in the U.S., and developing nations are rushing to emulate us. This condition is bound to cause prices to spiral higher until all the oil is gone.

Meanwhile, oil poisons us and destroys our planet. In the U.S., cars emit 20 percent of the fossil-fuel carbon dioxide that contributes to global warming; 34 percent of the nitrogen oxide that kills crops, lakes, and forests when it turns into acid rain; and 27 percent of the hydrocarbons that ruin our lungs with ozone smog. Diesels, home heating, and smokestack exhaust from utilities and oil and chemical plants produce even greater amounts. And every year, thousands of oil and gasoline spills make life impossible in waterways, pollute drinking water, and cost billions of dollars in cleanups and fire losses.

Coal is an even worse air polluter. And nuclear power is dying because spent nuclear fuel, which stays radioactive for fifty thousand years, cannot be disposed of safely, and because even the billions spent to build "fail-safe" backup systems cannot prevent catastrophic accidents. Also, oil, coal, and nuclear fires all promote global warming by adding to the total amount of heat in the atmosphere.

But clean, renewable energy alternatives like photovoltaic, solar-thermal, wind, small hydroelectric, geothermal, ocean-thermal, and tide energies can combat all these problems simultaneously. Each is virtually pollution-free compared with fossil fuels. When used in conjunction with water electrolyzers, the energy produced by each of them can be converted into hydrogen, which produces almost no pollution at all when burned, and which can fuel everything from power plants to furnaces to automobiles. And none of them artificially adds heat to the atmosphere.

Renewables also afford the added benefit of strengthening our state's economy. By encouraging decentralization of energy production they bolster competition and create more local jobs, smoothing out the boom/bust cycle that oil fosters. They can free us from the need to buy fuel or energy from other states or countries, and from price spirals caused by increasing demands for oil. And any excess energy they produce can be exported.

All the technology needed to greatly expand the use of clean renewables is available, but it remains idle because of simple economics. Hydrogen fuel from photovoltaic arrays would cost about two dollars for an amount equivalent to a gallon of gasoline, and electricity from most renewable sources is a bit more expensive than that from coal-fired plants. But if downstream costs of fossil fuels and fission are included in the equation (medical costs of treating people who breathe dirty air; losses of crops, fish, and buildings to acid rain and fallout; the expense of protecting coastal areas from ocean levels that will rise because of the greenhouse effect; etc.) then renewables are already cheaper.

In light of these conditions, please support incentives that attract renewable energy companies to our state, increased funding for development of energy alternatives in our state, tax advantages for residents who buy renewable alternatives, and mandatory internalization of the downstream costs of fossil fuels and nuclear power.

Thank you for your consideration.

Sincerely,

—
—
—
—

———
———
———
———

RE: Establishing economic incentives for conservation

Dear

I am a taxpayer interested in protecting the environment. I am sending
this letter to urge you to introduce or lend your support to legislation that
provides tax breaks for manufacturers of energy-saving devices like solar
collectors and tax breaks for residents who add insulation, storm windows,
high-efficiency furnaces, etc., to their existing homes and businesses; and
provides requirements for the restructuring of vehicle licensing fees to
make them inversely proportional to mileage rates.

Even before 1990, when Saddam Hussein threw the world's oil-based
economy into turmoil, the U.S. trade deficit had grown to gigantic
proportions, largely because we import nearly half the oil we use. But the
consequences of that deficit, enormous though they may be, pale in
comparison to two other energy problems that face us today. One is
pollution. Smog, acid rain, and global warming—all largely attributable to
energy use—are rapidly destroying our environment. Many experts agree
that they have reached crisis stage around the world. The other problem is
oil depletion. The world's oil supply is projected to be virtually used up
during the next century.

Climatologists, ecologists, and economists agree that energy conservation is
one of our most potent weapons against these problems. I believe our state
should do its part to encourage conservation. Of course, conservation in
one state cannot solve global environmental and energy crises. Before that
can be accomplished, clean, renewable energy sources must also be
developed, and deforestation must be stopped and reforestation begun

around the world.   But I believe the measures I mentioned above must be adopted if we are to avert economic and environmental disaster, and I would be proud to see our state become a leader in adopting them.

Thank you for your consideration.

Sincerely,

—
—
—
—

—
—
—
—

RE: Banning chlorofluorocarbons and halons

Dear

While law enforcement agencies make every effort to keep illegal drugs out of our state, chemicals that may ultimately be even more destructive are being used legally. I refer to chlorofluorocarbons (or CFCs) and halons.

Scientists have now determined beyond all doubt that these chemicals are responsible for the destruction of the Earth's protective ozone layer. Studies show that as much as 6.2 percent of it is already gone, and the rate of deterioration is accelerating because the amount of CFCs and halons in the air is increasing and each molecule of them can destroy up to ten thousand molecules of ozone in the upper atmosphere.

As more of this protective layer disappears, more ultraviolet solar radiation will leak through to the Earth's surface, damaging living things, including human beings. Popular accounts have focused on the few thousand additional cases of skin cancer we are likely to see as a short-term consequence, but the problem is much more grave than that. There will probably be increases in cataracts and other signs of premature aging in humans and other animals; damage to immune systems; reductions in crop, timber, fish, and ranch yields; an upset of the fragile marine ecology; a decrease in the size of plant foliage; and, eventually, a general decline, perhaps a total collapse, of the Earth's entire biosphere.

As if that were not enough, these same CFCs and halons are also responsible for up to 20 percent of the greenhouse effect because they trap up to twenty thousand times as much solar heat as does an equal amount of carbon dioxide. And as greater volumes of them are released, that percentage—and the subsequent rate of global warming—will grow dramatically. So, even if efforts to replace fossil fuels with clean energy sources succeed, we still may soon face rising sea levels and an increase in the frequency and severity of storms unless we stop the emission of these substances.

Of course, the federal government showed its recognition of the problem years ago when it banned the use of CFCs as aerosol propellants throughout the U.S. But since that time their use in other applications has multiplied. And while some manufacturers and users have admitted the dangers and voluntarily opted to quit buying and selling them, many have not. The electronics industry employs them extensively as solvents. Hospitals use them as sterilants. Polystyrene and other plastic foams are full of them. Nearly every family in America now owns a refrigerator and/or air conditioner that uses them. And almost every molecule of them will eventually seep into the air. Halons are less ubiquitous, but are used in fire extinguishers, and so are released not accidentally, but by design.

More benign substitutes for CFCs and halons have been identified for virtually every application. They are at present less convenient and/or initially more costly, but they are necessary—the price of not switching to them is unconscionable. Some plans have already been made to phase these substitutes in, but I believe they are too little too late. The situation is much too serious to allow the possible economic consequences to any particular business to get in the way of immediately substituting safer chemicals.

Please help protect the environment by helping to solve this potentially devastating problem. I urge you to introduce and/or vote for bills designed to ban, statewide, the manufacture, distribution, and importation of CFCs and halons, and to encourage the development of safer alternatives through economic incentives such as income tax breaks for manufacturers and consumers of such alternatives.

Thank you for your consideration.

Sincerely,

—
—
—
—

—
—
—
—

RE: Establishing economic incentives for recycling

Dear

Like many residents of our state, I have grown very concerned about the environment. I believe that because we Americans cause more smog, acid rain, and greenhouse warming than anybody else, we should be doing more to combat these problems—not just for our own benefit, but for the benefit of our children and succeeding generations as well. And I know of no better way to begin than by doing more to promote the recycling of paper right here in our state.

Every year, 850 million trees are cut to make the 50 million tons of paper Americans use. Much of it comes from the disappearing rain forests that until recently have harbored half the world's plant and animal species and have helped prevent a runaway greenhouse effect by absorbing carbon dioxide and producing 40 percent of the oxygen in our atmosphere. A lot of it comes from timber cut from our own federal lands. Virtually all of it ends up in our landfills, exacerbating the problem cities face as they run out of room to dispose of solid wastes. Worse, the paper industry contributes greatly to smog, acid rain, and global warming because it is the largest single industrial user of fuel oil. And its processes use billions of gallons of our diminishing supply of clean water and create large amounts of deadly dioxin.

Every ton of recycled paper saves 17 trees, 7,000 gallons of water, and the equivalent of 4,100 kilowatt-hours of electricity or 380 gallons of oil— enough to heat the average home for six months. It also causes 35 percent less water pollution and up to 95 percent less air pollution, and keeps open as much landfill area as an "average" resident of our state uses in a year. And recycling creates jobs—five times as many people are needed to produce a ton of recycled paper as are needed to put out the same amount of product using virgin wood pulp.

But because of the U.S. Forest Service's policy of selling timber below cost (which indirectly subsidizes virgin-pulp production and discourages recycling), and because the timber and pulp industries aren't required to include downstream costs in prices for logs and virgin pulp, recycled paper is having a hard time competing. Consumers are hesitant to buy recycled paper products because they appear costlier, so manufacturers are reluctant to use recycled paper. As a result, discarded newspapers sit waiting for buyers while the recycled paper industry struggles to grow.

Together we can help to right this situation. I urge you to help save our environment by authoring or voting for legislation designed to tax products made from virgin wood pulp in order to provide tax credits for recycled products, and/or other legislation that will foster the growth of the recycled products industry.

Thank you for your consideration.

Sincerely,

—
—
—
—

—
—
—

—

RE: Adopting tough state emission standards

Dear

In my opinion, our state needs to adopt stringent air pollution standards. The exhausts from every vehicle and smokestack within its borders contribute to the world's growing air pollution problems, and those problems have reached crisis stage. Smog and acid rain are destroying forests, fisheries, and crops around the world. According to the EPA, over 76 million Americans are breathing air that does not meet the clean-air standards. And it is now clear that global warming is not a fanciful idea, but a harsh reality.

Vehicles are a large part of the problem. According to the Department of Transportation, each year an average car in the U.S. logs over ten thousand miles, burns over five hundred gallons of gasoline, and pumps over ten thousand pounds of carbon dioxide into the air. Cars emit 20 percent of the fossil-fuel carbon dioxide, 27 percent of the hydrocarbons, and 34 percent of the nitrogen oxides that go into the air in the U.S. Trucks and buses are even worse polluters than cars.

Chemical and oil plants and utilities are the sources of about half our nitrogen oxide and hydrocarbon pollutants. They also produce particulates and huge amounts of carbon dioxide, sulfur dioxide, and other harmful gases.

That these emissions must be reduced before smog, acid rain, and global warming can be brought into check is without question. But federal efforts to do this have historically been tardy and unfocused. The U.S. is still widely regarded as the world's most wasteful nation and its worst polluter. During the 1980s, clean-air regulations that were inadequate to begin with were relaxed or disregarded time after time, as federal officials bowed to the lobbying efforts of oil, chemical, and automobile companies, placing the profitability of those companies above the health of the environment and the American public. And federal clean-air legislation introduced in 1990 was too little too late to solve the problem.

But we can insist on clean air in our state. I urge you to introduce or support the adoption in our state of tough emission laws like those the state of California has pioneered. They should include provisions for mandatory heavy fines for industrial pollution and taxes on the manufacture and purchase of low-mileage vehicles; stipulations that the resultant revenues be funneled into the development of clean, renewable energy sources like solar power and hydrogen fuel that will ultimately reduce emissions; and safeguards to prevent business payoffs from killing these measures or undermining their effectiveness after they become law.

Please help our state join others that have already begun the fight against the ravages of air pollution. Every resident of this state and every living thing on this planet has a right to breathe clean air.

Thank you for your consideration.

Sincerely,

—
—
—
—

—

—

—

—

RE: Stiffer fines for oil spills, toxic dumping, etc.

Dear

Every week, more oil spills contaminate the Earth's waterways, more industrial effluent pours into our streams, more radioactivity is released into our air, more gasoline leaks into our drinking water from underground tanks, more toxic chemicals are spilled on our highways, and so on. So many hazardous substances are now being used that it is only a matter of time before our state falls victim to an environmental tragedy like those at Love Canal, Three Mile Island, and Prince William Sound.

Although the U.S. Environmental Protection Agency is supposed to prevent problems like this, it cannot. It operates on a yearly budget of $8.5 billion, but it would take $30 billion to clean up just the sites that have already been identified (and ignore the large majority that have not even been reported).

So the EPA compromises. It allows generators of less than one hundred kilograms of hazardous waste to dispose of it as if it were ordinary garbage, without paying any fines at all. Companies whose trucks, trains, or ships are involved in accidents are often not charged for spills of oil or other hazardous substances. Industrial polluters are usually simply asked to clean up their messes. If they refuse, they may or may not be prosecuted. If judges rule against them, they may or may not be forced to comply, but only after lengthy appeals, during which many continue to pollute. Occasionally an offender is charged a fine that amounts to only a slap on the wrist.

Instead, polluters should be held responsible for their actions. Offenders should immediately be enjoined from further discharges and heavily fined. If they fail to comply, they should be jailed and charged, and their assets seized for payment of their fines, just as they would be had they refused to pay their income taxes. Revenues from such fines should be used to pay not only cleanup costs, but also the expense of developing substitute products that are not hazardous.

Federal regulations have not kept spills and dumping of toxic and hazardous substances from occurring, nor have they resulted in nonhazardous alternatives. What is needed is better legislation at the state level. I ask that you work for the enactment of new state laws that shift the burden of preventing and cleaning up hazardous spills and toxic dump sites away from taxpayers and toward polluters; and that these laws include provisions to fine and tax polluters and funnel the resultant revenues into the development of alternatives that are not hazardous to humans or to the environment.

Thank you for your consideration.

Sincerely,

—
—
—
—

—
—
—
—

RE: Abandoning nuclear power

Dear

I am opposed to the exorbitant rates for electricity that nuclear power plants charge. I resent being contaminated. And I am sick of worrying that some human error or some software or hardware glitch might trigger a world-ending launch of nuclear warheads. Please join me in my effort to see nuclear-waste repositories and nuclear power in any form outlawed in our state.

Nuclear accidents cannot be prevented, regardless of how many billions of dollars are spent on "fail-safe" backup systems. Nuclear Regulatory Commission documents show that more than thirty-three thousand of them have occurred in U.S. power plants since the Three Mile Island disaster in 1979. A thousand of these are considered significant. Testifying before the Energy and Power Subcommittee of the House Committee on Energy and Commerce in 1986, NRC Commissioner James Asseltine suggested a serious accident is likely to occur in the U.S. within two decades. The probability of a major core-melt during that period has been put at 45 percent by an NRC projection.

Such an accident would be catastrophic. The Chernobyl accident in 1986 displaced 135,000 people from 179 villages; killed 31 people outright; irradiated so many that tens of thousands of cancer deaths, birth defects, and genetic mutations are expected; contaminated huge amounts of crops, livestock, and wildlife in several countries; and cost the Soviets $13 billion (including the loss of the power plant). An Atomic Energy Commission study done years ago estimated that a meltdown in the U.S. could injure 73,000 and kill 27,000, while causing $17 billion in property damage.

The so-called "inherently safe" reactors that have been proposed may be feasible to build decades from now, but even they are untenable, because we will still have no means of safely disposing of the spent fuel they generate.

Such waste already presents serious problems. Since it stays dangerously radioactive for fifty thousand years and cannot be safely disposed of, voters who don't want it near them defeat dump site proposals. As a result, it is only temporarily stored. By the year 2001 we may have seventy-two thousand tons of it in the United States. And by then we will also have enough low-level milling and mining waste to build a mound as high as a man's head from New York to Los Angeles.

If waste from fission reactors is dangerous, building the nuclear weapons they make possible is insane. As Carl Sagan and others have pointed out, a nuclear conflict cannot be won, because in addition to releasing deadly radiation, it would result in a "nuclear winter." According to the Department of Energy, U.S. laboratories and plants that make nuclear weapons have released radioactive isotopes on at least 155 occasions (no one knows how many instances have gone unreported). This pollution has probably caused thousands of cancers and birth defects in humans and an incalculable amount of damage to wildlife, and Congress has estimated that it will take up to $200 billion of our money over the next hundred years to clean it up. Nuclear weapons testing is credited with even greater damage. According to Dr. John Gofman, atomic testing has probably already condemned 1,116,000 people to developing lung cancer. Ironically, our nuclear weapons may already be obsolete; the threat of Soviet aggression, which they were designed to deter, seems to have disintegrated.

I believe atomic chain reactions belong on stars, not here. This planet is not big enough for both human beings and nuclear power. We must choose between them while we still have a choice. Please help us choose human beings by committing your effort and influence to a legislative measure that makes this state a "nuclear-free zone."

Thank you for your consideration.

Sincerely,

—
—
—
—

—

—

—

—

RE: More use of recycled paper by the government

Dear

I believe your office and the other state offices can do the environment a great service, very easily and rather painlessly, by simply reducing the amount of paper they use, buying more recycled paper (preferably "minimum-impact" off-white paper), and recycling more of their waste-paper.

Most paper is made from virgin wood pulp through processes which use, for every ton of paper, 28 million Btus of energy, 24,000 gallons of water, 360 pounds of salt cake, 216 pounds of lime, 76 pounds of soda ash, and 17 trees, and produce 176 pounds of solid waste and 120 pounds of air and water pollutants. This not only depletes valuable natural resources, but also contributes to erosion, smog, acid rain, global warming, deforestation, desertification, and the extinction of plant, animal, and insect species. And because we use most paper once and discard it, paper occupies a third of our overcrowded landfill space.

All of these problems can be combated simultaneously and forcefully by simply conserving and recycling paper. Recycling consumes no trees and up to 60 percent less water and 70 percent less energy; causes 35 percent less water pollution and up to 95 percent less air pollution; and creates five times as many jobs as virgin-pulp processing. Since it is the bleaching process that generates dioxin when paper is made from virgin pulp, recycling, which requires less bleaching, also creates less dioxin. And the production of minimum-impact off-white recycled paper is virtually dioxin-free.

That recycling is cost-effective is undeniable. Industries have profited from it for years, and now many municipalities and several states, awakened to the fact that recycling is the most efficient waste-management option available, have followed their lead. The Illinois state procurement agency, for instance, adopted policies in the summer of 1990 that require recycled paper and other recycled products be bought whenever possible. And Maryland has already saved enough energy by recycling to heat ten thousand homes for a year.

Despite its advantages, though, recycled paper struggles to compete because of lack of consumer demand. Even though it would be cheaper if below-cost Forest Service timber sales were discontinued and downstream costs of virgin-pulp pollution internalized, its market price makes it appear more expensive to the consumer. Consequently, consumers are reluctant to buy it, so manufacturers hesitate to use it—with the result that concerned citizens often collect more wastepaper than can be used, while sales of recycled products remain slow.

What is needed to break this impasse is a large demand for recycled paper, and I think our state government should help provide this demand by printing more of the thousands of tax forms, brochures, letters, and other documents generated by state offices on recycled paper and by using recycled paper in other areas. I see no good reason for not eventually using it in every state application from highway department toilet tissue to supreme court documents if it will help save the world's forests and slow pollution and global warming.

I urge you to direct your office staff to conserve paper, use more recycled paper, and recycle their wastepaper; and I ask that you draft or support a bill that encourages each of the various state agencies to do the same.

Thank you for your consideration.

Sincerely,

—
—
—
—

—
—
—
—
—

RE: Use of renewable energy by the government

Dear

I believe our state should begin employing more energy conservation
measures and more clean, renewable, alternative energy sources like solar
power, wind power, and electrolytic hydrogen in each new government
installation, whether it be a new prison building, new highway lighting, or
the remodeling of a university.

The Chernobyl disaster and the insoluble problem of what to do with
nuclear waste have proved that nuclear fission is too dangerous to continue
using. Fossil fuels cause smog, acid rain, and global warming, and will be
depleted within a few decades. Both threaten to virtually destroy our
environment, and both require huge, centralized power generation stations
to produce electricity (and/or fuel), which are easy targets for terrorists.
And neither provides a stable foundation for our economy.

But clean, renewable energy alternatives like photovoltaic, solar-thermal,
wind, small hydroelectric, geothermal, ocean-thermal, and tide energies can
never be depleted. They produce virtually no pollution. When used in
conjunction with water electrolyzers, the energy produced by each of them
can be converted into hydrogen, which produces almost no pollution at all
when burned, and which can be used to fuel everything from power plants
to furnaces to automobiles. And they encourage decentralization, even
complete energy independence—which translates into better security and a
hedge against inflation.

We already possess all the technology needed to begin using more clean,
renewable energy, but we have failed to do so because of simple economics.
Hydrogen fuel from photovoltaic arrays would cost about two dollars for an
amount equivalent to a gallon of gasoline, and electricity from most
renewable sources is a bit more expensive than that from coal-fired
plants. But if downstream costs of fossil fuels and nuclear fission are
included in the equation (medical costs of treating people who breathe
dirty air; losses of crops, fish, and buildings to acid rain and fallout; storm
damage resulting from global warming; etc.), renewables are already more
cost-effective.

Since governments end up paying a large percentage of these downstream costs, and since they are concerned with long-term rather than short-term investments, they actually lose money by not using more renewables (and compromise their own security, the environment, and public health at the same time). By not using more renewables, governments in effect subsidize smog, acid rain, global warming, radioactive contamination, dependence on foreign oil, the depletion of natural resources, mass migrations during oil booms, and escalating trade deficits.

The most expeditious way to remedy this situation is to immediately begin including conservation and clean, renewable energy use in all new government designs. For instance, architects should be instructed to include solar collectors, photovoltaic modules, and wind generators in their designs for new state buildings and remodeling projects. Highway engineers should call for solar lighting at illuminated intersections. State offices should coordinate car pools for their employees. And so on.

I urge you to endorse more use of energy conservation measures and clean, renewable energy alternatives in every possible application in our state. Let's speed up the inevitable process of phasing in clean, renewable energy and phasing out fossil fuels and nuclear power, instead of waiting until we are forced, by crises, to do so hastily.

Thank you for your consideration.

Sincerely,

—
—
—
—

Chapter 9

Letters to County Officials

If you live anywhere in the United States other than Louisiana (which has parishes instead of counties), Alaska, the District of Columbia, or one of the forty-four independent cities (most of which are small towns in Virginia), you live in a county governed by county commissioners and/or other county officials. The letters in this chapter were written especially for these officials, to raise environmental issues that usually need to be dealt with at the county level.

Letter 86 asks that the county establish a permanent hazardous-waste collection center to keep hazardous materials out of landfills. You probably won't need this letter if your county already has such a facility.

Letter 87 asks county officials to provide another permanent facility for collecting and recycling chlorofluorocarbons.

Letter 88 asks that more trees be planted along county roads and on other county property.

Letter 89 requests that your county discontinue the salting of roads.

Letter 90 suggests energy conservation measures and clean, renewable energy sources be designed into new county facilities.

Letter 91 suggests your county be declared a "nuclear-free zone."

Letter 92 asks county officials to reduce and recycle county-government paper.

To obtain names and addresses for county officials, I suggest you call your county clerk or stop by your county courthouse. Failing that, you may wish to call your city administration offices (city hall), or ask a reference librarian at your local library or an officer of a voter organization. Don't forget to ask for the appropriate titles and greetings so that you can show your respect—and so that your letter will be taken seriously.

If you live in Louisiana, you may want to use these letters as guides for writing your own, substituting "parish" for "county." If you live in an independent city, you may want to skip to chapter 10.

—
—
—
—

RE: Establishing hazardous waste facilities

Dear

I believe it is imperative that our county establish a permanent facility for collecting and properly disposing of hazardous wastes.

The amount of hazardous waste generated by Americans every year amounts to more than two thousand pounds per person. Much of it is disposed of in ordinary landfills. Up to a quarter of it is composed of household wastes like batteries containing lead, cadmium, and/or mercury (about ten per person each year), paint and paint products containing heavy metals and solvents, mothballs, oven cleaners, explosives, insecticides, herbicides, rodenticides, fungicides, flammables, acids, drain cleaners, furniture polish and strippers, motor oil, and even radioactive smoke detectors. And since EPA regulations allow industries that generate less than one hundred kilograms of hazardous waste per month to dispose of their wastes in landfills, they often include highly toxic, flammable, corrosive, and/or explosive industrial chemicals as well.

Much of what does not go to landfills is poured into sewers. This includes an estimated average of ten ounces of recyclable motor oil (enough to spoil seventy-eight thousand gallons of drinking water) for every man, woman, and child each year, and an unknown quantity of antifreeze, flammable solvents, insecticides, rat poisons, etc. Still more hazardous waste is simply dumped on the ground in places where it endangers water supplies.

Landfills are not built to handle hazardous materials. Neither are sewer systems. And neither are highway verges, mine shafts, vacant lots, or streams. Inevitably, hazardous wastes disposed of in these places harm wildlife, and eventually contaminate the soil and aquifers that are the sources of our own food and water supplies. And once they are contaminated, they may remain unusable for decades or centuries.

But until permanent, convenient facilities are set up to allow for the proper disposal of hazardous waste, people will continue this unnecessary polluting, and our own health and the health of our environment will suffer the ever-worsening cumulative effects—including cancer, birth defects, and genetic damage.

I urge you to help protect our environment and the health of the citizens of our county by taking action now to establish permanent, safe, convenient hazardous-waste collection and disposal facilities.

Thank you for your consideration.

Sincerely,

—
—
—
—

_____, 199_   #87

__

__

__

__

RE: Establishing a CFC recovery facility

Dear

I believe our county should establish a facility to collect and recycle
chlorofluorocarbons (CFCs), and adopt measures to ensure that these
chemicals are not released into the environment.

Scientists have determined beyond all doubt that CFCs are largely
responsible for the destruction of the Earth's protective ozone layer.
Studies show that as much as 6.2 percent of the ozone layer is already
gone, and the rate of deterioration is accelerating because the amount of
CFCs in the air is increasing (each CFC molecule can destroy up to ten
thousand molecules of ozone in the upper atmosphere).

As more of this protective ozone layer disappears, more ultraviolet solar
radiation will leak through to the Earth's surface, damaging living things,
including humans. Popular accounts have focused on the few thousand
additional cases of skin cancer we are likely to see as a short-term
consequence, but the problem is much more grave than that. There will
probably be increases in cataracts and other signs of premature aging in
humans and other animals; damage to immune systems; reductions in
crop, timber, fish, and ranch yields; an upset of the fragile marine ecology;
a decrease in the size of plant foliage; and eventually a general decline,
perhaps a total collapse, of the entire biosphere.

As if that were not enough, CFCs also contribute to the greenhouse effect
because they trap up to twenty thousand times as much solar heat as does
an equal amount of carbon dioxide. And as greater volumes of them are
released, the rate of global warming will grow dramatically. So even if
efforts to replace fossil fuels with clean energy sources succeed, we still
will soon face rising sea levels and an increase in the frequency and
severity of storms unless we stop releasing CFCs.

Of course, the use of CFCs as aerosol propellants was banned in the U.S. years ago. But their use has multiplied in other areas. And while some manufacturers and users have admitted the danger and voluntarily opted to discontinue their use, many have not. Nearly every family in America owns a refrigerator and/or air conditioner that uses them. And when these are serviced or discarded, CFCs can leak into the air.

Beginning in 1992, federal legislation will require some large service shops to recover CFC refrigerant gases using "vampire" machines that suck them out of refrigeration coils, but smaller shops and private individuals will continue to go unregulated. This means that thousands of pounds of these chemicals will continue to be released into the Earth's atmosphere every year when refrigerators, chillers, freezers, air conditioners, cars, and vapor degreasers are serviced or discarded. And it means that equipment that has already been discarded will continue to leak CFCs as it deteriorates. By the year 2000, or 2010, which is when the United States and ninety-two other nations have agreed in principle that CFCs will finally be eliminated, irreparable damage will have been done to the environment.

I believe each of us has a responsibility to our children and to future generations to do what we can to help prevent the environmental catastrophe that CFCs are now contributing to. I think local governments should take it upon themselves to finish the job the U.S. Congress started (but was unable to complete because of pressure from big business) by passing and enforcing laws that work in cases where federal rules fall short, and by providing local recycling facilities. I strongly urge you to work to establish a CFC recovery and recycling facility in our county and to support measures that prohibit CFCs from being emitted into the atmosphere within its borders.

Thank you for your consideration.

Sincerely,

___

___

___

___

—
—
—
—

RE: Planting trees on county property

Dear

I am writing to ask you to support and encourage the volunteer planting of more trees along roads, on the grounds of county buildings, and on other county-owned land.

Trees are vital to the health of the biosphere. They prevent a runaway greenhouse effect by absorbing carbon dioxide, stabilize soil, provide humidification and evaporative cooling (as much as ten degrees in urban areas), and emit the major portion of the oxygen we breathe. They also give us food, wood, shade, and beauty, and they shelter the majority of the Earth's plant, animal, and insect species.

Unfortunately, we have been cutting trees down at an escalating rate for so many centuries that we now stand on the brink of environmental catastrophe. We are razing the 70 million-year-old tropical rain forests that produce 40 percent of the oxygen in the air at the rate of 51 acres per minute, and are leaving behind eroding deserts. Our rain forests may all be gone by the year 2032. About 87 percent of the original ancient forests in the northwestern U.S. are already gone. Canada cuts 247,000 more acres of trees than it replants every year. And all over the world trees are constantly being bulldozed for farms, buildings, highways, and parking lots, and never replaced.

This deforestation is one of the reasons carbon dioxide, which traps solar heat and creates a greenhouse effect, has reached such a high concentration in our atmosphere that global warming has begun. Average global temperatures are already about half a degree higher than they were a century ago, and they could rise by as much as nine degrees in the next few decades, melting the Earth's ice caps, flooding coastal areas, turning farmland into deserts, and spawning frequent, violent storms.

This greenhouse effect is progressive. Even if we stop burning gasoline and coal to prevent more carbon dioxide from building up in the atmosphere, global warming will continue for years unless we do something to remove the carbon dioxide already in the air—something like planting more trees.

Were we able to grow enough trees, we could stabilize our atmosphere and bring global warming to a halt, buying ourselves some time to develop alternative fuels. Of course a project of that magnitude is far beyond the ability of any county or even any nation. But every tree planted, regardless of its location, helps reduce the level of carbon dioxide in the air a little bit, thereby slowing the greenhouse effect.

Grassroots tree-planting projects have already begun all over the world. The American Forestry Association's Global Releaf program, for instance, which began on Arbor Day, 1989, is helping Americans plant 100 million trees by 1992. But more government involvement is needed. Every local government needs to pitch in and do its share, by designing more trees into government building projects, by aiding volunteer efforts at reforestation and education, by publicly endorsing tree planting, and by sponsoring tree plantings by individual volunteers and organizations like the Boy Scouts of America.

Please join those of us who support reforestation by publicly endorsing it and by working to see that seedlings and guidelines are provided to any individual or group wishing to plant trees on county property.

Thank you for your consideration.

Sincerely,

—
—
—
—

—
—
—
—

RE: Discontinuing the salting of roads and bridges

Dear

It seems to me that our environment is besieged enough by contamination from leaking landfills, automobile exhaust, agricultural chemicals, and industrial wastes. Why must we spread tons of another harmful substance around nearly every time it snows?

Road salt is destructive. It kills most species of plants, retards the growth of fish eggs and fry in lakes, and retards the mixing of upper and lower layers of lake water that promotes the growth of bottom-dwelling invertebrates. It eats away car bodies, deteriorates road surfaces, corrodes bridges, and attacks underground cables and pipelines. It even taints groundwater, as many Massachusetts residents discovered when they had to close down nine municipal wells and one hundred private wells because of road-salt contamination. And once the cost of all this damage is factored into the price of road salt, the $25 per ton most street departments pay increases 6,400 percent to a whopping $1,600 per ton!

Clearly, alternatives are needed. And many exist. Some communities use dark cinders, which increase traction and aid melting by absorbing sunlight. Others are trying a special paving material that inhibits icing. In some mountainous areas where constant snowplowing renders additives useless, snow-tire/chain laws and driver education work well to keep traffic flowing.

I want you to know that I support the abandonment of salting as a means of clearing snowy roadways in our county, even if no alternative method of clearing is adopted.

Thank you for your consideration.

Sincerely,

—
—
—
—

—
—
—
—

RE: Energy conservation and renewable energy

Dear

I believe our county should begin employing more energy conservation
measures and more clean, renewable, alternative energy sources like solar
power, wind power, and electrolytic hydrogen in each new government
project, whether it be a new jail or the remodeling of an existing county
office.

The Chernobyl disaster and the insoluble problem of what to do with
nuclear wastes have proved that nuclear fission is too dangerous. Fossil
fuels cause smog, acid rain, and global warming, and they will be depleted
within a few decades. Both threaten to virtually destroy our environment,
and both require huge, centralized power-generation stations to produce
electricity (and/or fuel), which are easy targets for terrorists. And neither
provides a stable foundation for our economy.

But clean, renewable energy alternatives like photovoltaic, solar-thermal,
wind, small hydroelectric, geothermal, ocean-thermal, and tide energies can
never be depleted. They produce virtually no pollution. When used in
conjunction with water electrolyzers, the energy produced by each of them
can be converted into hydrogen, which produces almost no pollution at all
when burned, and which can be used to fuel everything from power plants
to furnaces to automobiles. And they encourage decentralization, even
complete energy independence—which translates into a hedge against
inflation.

All the technology needed to begin using more clean, renewable energy is
available. Costs are high; hydrogen fuel from photovoltaic arrays would
cost about two dollars for an amount equivalent to a gallon of gasoline, and
electricity from most renewable sources is a bit more expensive than that
from coal-fired plants. However, if downstream costs of fossil fuels and
nuclear fission are included in the equation (medical costs of treating
people who breathe dirty air; losses of crops, fish, and buildings to acid
rain and fallout; storm damage resulting from global warming; etc.),
renewables are already more cost-effective.

Growth of energy alternatives in the private sector has been much more sluggish than it could be because business is driven by short-term profits. But since governments are concerned with the public welfare and long-term stability, clean, renewable energy and conservation should be far more appealing to them than to business.

I believe all governments, including our county government, should begin including energy conservation and clean, renewable energy use in all new designs and purchases. For instance, architects should be instructed to include solar collectors, photovoltaic modules, and wind generators in their designs for new county buildings and remodeling projects; county officials should coordinate car pools for county employees; the county should only purchase vehicles that get superior gas mileage; and so on.

I urge you to endorse more use of energy conservation measures and clean, renewable energy alternatives in every possible application in our country. Let's accelerate the inevitable process of phasing in clean, renewable energy and phasing out fossil fuels and nuclear power, instead of waiting until we are forced, by crises, to do so hastily.

Thank you for your consideration.

Sincerely,

—
—
—
—

RE: Declaring our county a "nuclear-free zone"

Dear

Like many other residents of our county, I am opposed to nuclear arms and nuclear power plants. I am writing today to ask you to help ensure that no form of nuclear power will ever be allowed in this county.

Nuclear accidents cannot be prevented, regardless of how many billions of dollars are spent on "fail-safe" backup systems. Nuclear Regulatory Commission documents show that more than thirty-three thousand of them have occurred in U.S. power plants since the 1979 incident at Three Mile Island. A thousand of these are considered significant. Testifying before the Energy and Power Subcommittee of the House Committee on Energy and Commerce in 1986, NRC Commissioner James Asseltine suggested that a serious accident is likely in the U.S. within the next two decades. The probability of a major core-melt during that period has been put at 45 percent by an NRC projection.

Such an accident would be catastrophic. The Chernobyl debacle in 1986 displaced 135,000 people from 179 villages; killed 31 people outright; irradiated so many that tens of thousands of cancer deaths, birth defects, and genetic mutations are expected; contaminated huge amounts of crops, livestock, and wildlife in several countries; and cost the Soviets $13 billion (including the loss of the power plant). An Atomic Energy Commission study done years ago estimated that a meltdown in the U.S. could injure 73,000 and kill 27,000, while causing $17 billion in property damage.

The so-called "inherently safe" reactors that have been proposed may be feasible to build decades from now, but even they are untenable because we will still have no means of safely disposing of the spent fuel they will generate.

Such waste already presents serious problems. Since it stays dangerously radioactive for fifty thousand years and cannot be safely disposed of, voters who don't want it near them defeat dump-site proposals. As a result, the waste is temporarily stored. By the year 2001 we may have seventy-two thousand tons of it in the United States. And by that time we will also have enough low-level milling and mining waste to build a mound as high as a man's head from New York to Los Angeles.

If waste from fission reactors is dangerous, building the nuclear weapons they make possible is insane. As Carl Sagan and others have pointed out, a nuclear conflict cannot be won because in addition to releasing deadly radiation, it would result in a "nuclear winter."

The nuclear weapons industry has already wreaked havoc on public health. According to the U.S. Department of Energy, American laboratories and plants that make nuclear weapons have released radioactive isotopes on at least 155 occasions (no one knows how many instances have not been reported). This pollution has probably caused thousands of cancers and birth defects in humans and an incalculable amount of damage to wildlife, and Congress has estimated that it will cost up to $200 billion over the next hundred years to clean it up. Nuclear weapons testing is credited with even greater damage. According to Dr. John Gofman, atomic testing has probably already condemned 1,116,000 people to developing lung cancer. Ironically, our nuclear weapons may already be obsolete; the threat of Soviet aggression, which they were designed to deter, seems to have disintegrated.

Let's not wait until tens of thousands of Americans are killed by a meltdown, or tens of millions by a nuclear war triggered by some software or hardware malfunction. Let's put a stop to nuclear power now. Let's begin right here at home by making nuclear power and nuclear waste illegal in our county.

Thank you for your consideration.

Sincerely,

—
—
—
—

—
—
—
—

RE: More use of recylced paper by the county

Dear

I believe your office and the other county offices can do the environment a great service, very easily and rather painlessly, by simply reducing the amount of paper they use, buying more recycled paper (preferably "minimum-impact" off-white paper), and recycling more of their waste paper.

Most paper is made from virgin wood pulp by processes which use for every ton of paper, 28 million Btus of energy, 24,000 gallons of water, 360 pounds of salt cake, 216 pounds of lime, 76 pounds of soda ash, and 17 trees; and produce 176 pounds of solid waste and 120 pounds of air and water pollutants (including deadly dioxin and furans). This not only depletes valuable natural resources, but also contributes to erosion, smog, acid rain, global warming, deforestation, desertification, and the extinction of plant, animal, and insect species. And because we use most paper once and discard it, paper occupies a third of our overcrowded landfill space.

All of these problems can be combated simultaneously and forcefully by simply conserving and recycling paper. Recycling consumes no trees and up to 60 percent less water and 70 percent less energy; causes 35 percent less water pollution and up to 95 percent less air pollution; and creates five times as many jobs as virgin-pulp processing. Since it is the bleaching process that generates dioxin when paper is made from virgin pulp, recycling, which requires less bleaching, creates less dioxin. And the production of minimum-impact off-white recycled paper is virtually dioxin-free.

That recycling is cost-effective is undeniable. Industries have profited from it for years, and now many municipalities and several states, awakened to the fact that recycling is the most efficient waste-management option available, have followed their lead. Maryland, for instance, has saved enough energy by recycling to heat ten thousand homes for a year.

Despite its advantages, though, recycled paper struggles to compete because of lack of consumer demand. Even though it would be cheaper if below-cost Forest Service timber sales were discontinued and downstream costs of virgin-pulp pollution internalized, its market price makes it appear more costly to the consumer. Consequently, consumers are reluctant to buy it, so manufacturers hesitate to use it—with the result that concerned citizens often collect more wastepaper than can be used, while sales of recycled products remain slow.

What is needed to break this impasse is a large demand for recycled paper, and I believe all levels of government should help to provide this demand by specifying recycled paper for all applications from toilet tissue to court dockets.

I urge you to direct your office staff to conserve paper, use more recycled paper, and recycle wastepaper; and I ask that you work to encourage other county offices to do the same.

Thank you for your consideration.

Sincerely,

—
—
—
—

Chapter 10

Letters to Community Officials

The letters in this last chapter were written especially for mayors, city managers, city commissioners, town councilpersons, and others who may hold office in your community.

Letter 93 asks that a permanent curbside recycling program be established in your community.

Letter 94 asks for a permanent composting facility.

Letter 95 urges officials to begin designing a new mass-transit system.

Letter 96 concerns energy conservation and renewable energy alternatives.

Letter 97 asks that the salting of streets and bridges be discontinued.

Letter 98 suggests your community be declared a "nuclear-free zone."

Letter 99 asks community leaders to cooperate with county officials to establish hazardous-waste facilities.

Finally, letter 100 is a plea for more trees to be planted in your community.

Chances are good that you either know some city officials personally or that you know a lot about them from local newspaper, radio, and television

stories. If not, you can easily obtain their names and addresses by calling your city hall (or equivalent), which is usually listed in your telephone directory under the name of your city. Or you can ask a reference librarian, a local voter organization, or a secretary at your local courthouse. Be sure to ask for the right title and greeting, since using them may make a difference in how much consideration is given to your requests (letters to mayors, for example, are customarily addressed in the form: The Honorable John Smith, Mayor of [your city, your state]).

If you live in a rural area, you may want to send some of these letters to officials of a community you trade in.

Local governments differ so widely in terms of how many people hold authority, who is responsible for what, etc., that these letters cannot be tailored to a specific office or even a specific number of offices. You may wish either to use these letters as guides for writing letters of your own or to add specific postscripts to make them more clearly applicable to your community.

—
—
—
—

RE: Curbside recycling

Dear

The amount of resources our "disposable society" wastes in landfills is mind-boggling. Every year Americans generate enough waste to fill 145,000 miles of garbage trucks. We use enough glass bottles and jars to fill the World Trade Center's two skyscrapers twenty-six times and enough plastic bottles to fill a four hundred-mile-long caravan of dump trucks. We discard 100 billion pounds of wastepaper every year, along with as much iron and steel as our automobile industry uses, enough aluminum to rebuild all our commercial airplanes four times, 300 billion pounds of compostable grass clippings, leaves, etc., and forty-one times as much motor oil as was spilled in Prince William Sound by the Exxon Valdez.

All these commodities are valuable resources. Compost, for instance, is highly valued as a substitute for expensive chemical fertilizers, and last year Americans earned nearly a billion dollars by collecting discarded aluminum cans.

Recycling can save enormous amounts of resources and keep huge quantities of pollutants out of the environment. Recycling "tin" cans, for instance, saves 74 percent of the energy needed to make them from scratch, and causes 76 percent less water pollution and 85 percent less air pollution. Recycling a ton of aluminum cans saves 177 million Btus of energy, 8,766 pounds of bauxite, 1,020 pounds of petroleum coke, 966 pounds of soda ash, 327 pounds of pitch, and 238 pounds of lime; and keeps 3,290 pounds of red mud, 789 pounds of solid waste, and 76 pounds of air pollutants out of the environment. Recycling a ton of wastepaper can save 19 million Btus of energy, 7,000 gallons of water, 360 pounds of salt cake, 216 pounds of lime, 76 pounds of soda ash, 17 trees, and 3 cubic yards of landfill space; and keep up to 60 pounds of air and water pollutants, including deadly dioxins and furans, out of the environment (producing recycled paper also creates up to five times as many jobs as making paper from virgin wood pulp).

As much as 86 percent of American household refuse can be recycled to produce revenue, yet we only recycle about 10 percent. We pay an average of $65 per ton to bury the rest in landfills, where it may last for hundreds or thousands of years. But a third of U.S. landfills will be full this year, and we are running out of places to put the five hundred new ones that are needed annually.

What we are doing, essentially, is indirectly subsidizing smog, acid rain, global warming, deforestation, the extinction of plant and animal species, and the pollution of our drinking water, while at the same time running out of space for landfills and unnecessarily accelerating the depletion of natural resources. That makes about as much sense as burning money and inhaling the smoke! What we should be doing instead is recycling as much as possible, and profiting, both economically and environmentally, from the savings.

Japan recycles up to 51 percent of its waste, and some European cities recycle 65 percent. Curbside recycling is the most effective method of waste management, which is why over six hundred American communities use it. Perkasie, Pennsylvania, saved 40 percent on disposal and 30 percent on collection, and cut its trash volume in half the very first year it began its program of picking up recyclables for free while charging to pick up other trash. And in just the first two years of its beverage-container recycling program, New York saved between $119 million and $169 million in solid waste disposal, cleanup, and energy costs, and created thirty-eight hundred new jobs.

I am tired of watching our community pollute the environment by throwing away resources. I urge you to do everything in your power to promote the establishment of a permanent, comprehensive curbside recycling program here as soon as possible.

Thank you for your consideration.

Sincerely,

—
—
—
—

—
—
—
—

RE: Establishing a permanent composting program

Dear

I think our community needs to do more to protect the environment. I believe establishing a permanent, community-wide composting program would be an excellent way to begin.

As you surely know, landfills everywhere are closing because they are full, or because overuse and other factors are causing leachates from them to contaminate water supplies. There were over eighteen thousand landfills in the United States in 1970. By 1980, that figure had shrunk to nine thousand, and it now stands at six thousand. By the end of this year, half of American cities must use new landfills. Yet we continue to bury 24 million tons of leaves and grass clippings in landfills every year, while buying millions of tons of dirt, peat moss, and fertilizers for our lawns and gardens instead of using compost. Each fall, 75 percent of America's solid waste is leaves. Also, sewage treatment is becoming an evermore expensive and difficult problem all over the country, yet we continue to flush enormous quantities of vegetable peelings down our garbage disposals.

In all, between 15 percent and 30 percent of municipal waste is biodegradable yard waste and vegetable scraps well suited for composting. And composting makes sense. While disposal in landfills costs an average of $65 per ton of waste, disposal in municipal compost heaps costs only about $35. Woodbury, New Jersey, and Davis, California, have combined composting and curbside recycling to cut their solid waste disposal volumes in half. At least eighty other New Jersey towns have turned to composting programs (dumping leaves in landfills is no longer allowed anywhere in New Jersey). And in all, there are more than 651 composting programs in 29 states.

I urge you to do everything you can to help establish a permanent composting facility and the curbside pickup of organic materials in our community.

Thank you for your consideration.

Sincerely,

__

__

__

__

—
—
—
—

RE: A mass-transit system

Dear

I believe it is time for our community to begin designing a new mass-transit system—hopefully one that uses a clean, renewable energy alternative. My reasons are as follows:

Our environment is in terrible trouble. Acid rain has already killed half the red spruce trees in some European and U.S. forests, and thousands of lakes in the U.S., Canada, Norway, and other countries. The U.S. Environmental Protection Agency estimates that over 76 million of us are breathing air that does not meet its clean-air standards. And climatologists are predicting that greenhouse warming will raise global average temperatures by as much as nine degrees in the next few decades, which could flood coastal areas, turn arable land into desert, and increase the frequency and severity of storms.

Automobiles are a major cause of these problems. Every day, the 140 million cars in this country burn 200 million gallons of gasoline and emit 4 billion pounds of the carbon dioxide that is largely responsible for global warming. They also emit 34 percent of the nitrogen oxide that is a major cause of acid rain, and 27 percent of the hydrocarbons that result in the ozone smog that damages our lungs and kills vegetation in urban areas.

American cars carry an average of only 1.3 people. If only 2 percent of us were to leave our cars at home one day a week, we could save 84 million gallons of gasoline and keep 1.68 billion pounds of carbon dioxide out of the air every year. And if we could increase the fuel efficiency of our cars by just 1.7 miles per gallon, we would save more fuel than we could ever obtain from Arctic drilling.

Trains, subways, buses, even Hovercraft have been proven time and again to be far more fuel-efficient than cars, and therefore better for the environment. And of course they alleviate much of the traffic congestion that wastes fully 5 percent of our gasoline and creates parking problems in all urban areas. Clearly, in any sizable community, mass transit is needed. And we need not settle for smoke-belching diesel systems. Cleaner alternatives are available. For instance, Daimler-Benz has developed buses that burn hydrogen, the same virtually nonpolluting fuel used in our space shuttle's main engine.

Please help our community advance into the twentieth century before the twenty-first century begins. Push for a mass-transit system based on solar-powered or hydrogen-powered vehicles, or at least one that uses electricity, alcohol, natural gas, or some other fuel that is cleaner than diesel fuel or gasoline.

Thank you for your consideration.

Sincerely,

—
—
—
—

—
—
—
—

RE: Energy conservation and renewable energy

Dear

I believe our community should begin employing more energy conservation measures and more clean, renewable, alternative energy sources like solar power, wind power, and electrolytic hydrogen in each new government project, whether it be the acquisition of a new police car or the remodeling of a city office.

The Chernobyl disaster and the insoluble problem of what to do with nuclear wastes have proved that nuclear fission is too dangerous. Fossil fuels cause smog, acid rain, and global warming, and will be depleted within a few decades. Both of these energy sources threaten to virtually destroy our environment, and both require huge, centralized power-generation stations to produce electricity (and/or fuel), which are easy targets for terrorists. And neither provides a stable foundation for our economy.

But clean, renewable energy alternatives like photovoltaic, solar-thermal, wind, small hydroelectric, geothermal, ocean-thermal, and tide energies can never be depleted. They produce virtually no pollution. When used in conjunction with water electrolyzers, the energy produced by each of them can be converted into hydrogen, which produces almost no pollution at all when burned, and which can be used to fuel everything from power plants to furnaces to automobiles. And they encourage decentralization, even complete energy independence—which translates into a hedge against inflation.

All the technology needed to begin using more clean, renewable energy is available. Costs are high; hydrogen fuel from photovoltaic arrays would cost about two dollars for an amount equivalent to a gallon of gasoline, and electricity from most renewable sources is a bit more expensive than that from coal-fired plants. But if downstream costs of fossil fuels and nuclear fission are included in the equation (medical costs of treating people who breathe dirty air; losses of crops, fish, and buildings to acid rain and fallout; storm damage resulting from global warming; etc.) renewables are already more cost-effective.

Because business is driven by short-term profits, growth of energy alternatives in the private sector has been much more sluggish than it could be. But since governments are concerned with the public welfare and long-term stability, clean, renewable energy and conservation should be far more appealing to them than to business.

I believe all governments, including the one that serves our community, should begin including energy conservation and clean, renewable energy use in all new designs and purchases. For instance, architects should be instructed to include solar collectors, photovoltaic modules, and wind generators in their designs for new official buildings and remodeling projects, official vehicles should be purchased on the basis of gas mileage or alternate fuels, and so on.

I urge you to endorse more use of energy conservation measures and clean, renewable energy alternatives in every possible application in our community. Let's speed up the inevitable process of phasing in clean, renewable energy and phasing out fossil fuels and nuclear power, instead of waiting until we are forced, by crises, to do so hastily.

Thank you for your consideration.

Sincerely,

—
—
—
—

—
—
—
—

RE: Discontinuing the salting of streets and bridges

Dear

It seems to me that our environment is besieged enough by contamination from leaking landfills, automobile exhaust, agricultural chemicals, and industrial wastes. Why must we spread tons of another harmful substance around nearly every time it snows?

Road salt is destructive. It kills most species of plants and retards the growth of fish eggs and fry. It eats away car bodies, deteriorates road surfaces, corrodes bridges, and attacks underground cables and pipelines. It even taints groundwater, as many Massachusetts residents discovered when they had to close down nine municipal wells and one hundred private wells because of road-salt contamination. And once the cost of all this damage is factored into the price of road salt, the $25 per ton most street departments pay increases 6,400 percent to a whopping $1,600 per ton!

Clearly, alternatives are needed. And many exist. Some communities use dark cinders, which increase traction and aid melting by absorbing sunlight. Others are trying a special paving material that inhibits icing. In some mountainous areas where constant snowplowing renders additives useless, snow-tire/chain laws and driver education work well to keep traffic flowing.

I want you to know that I support the abandonment of salting as a means of clearing snowy streets in our community, even if no alternative method of clearing is adopted.

Thank you for your consideration.

Sincerely,

—
—
—
—

—
—
—
—

RE: Declaring our community a "nuclear-free zone"

Dear

Like many other residents of our community, I am opposed to nuclear arms
and nuclear power plants. I am writing today to ask you to help ensure
that no form of nuclear power will ever be allowed here.

Nuclear accidents cannot be prevented, regardless of how many billions of
dollars are spent on "fail-safe" backup systems. Nuclear Regulatory
Commission documents show that more than thirty-three thousand of
them have occurred in U.S. power plants since the 1979 incident at Three
Mile Island. A thousand of these are considered significant. Testifying
before the Energy and Power Subcommittee of the House Committee on
Energy and Commerce in 1986, NRC Commissioner James Asseltine
suggested that a serious accident is likely in the U.S. within the next two
decades. The probability of a major core-melt during that period has been
put at 45 percent by an NRC projection.

Such an accident would be catastrophic. The Chernobyl debacle in 1986
displaced 135,000 people from 179 villages; killed 31 people outright;
irradiated so many that tens of thousands of cancer deaths, birth defects,
and genetic mutations are expected; contaminated huge amounts of crops,
livestock, and wildlife in several countries; and cost the Soviets $13 billion
(including the loss of the power plant). An Atomic Energy Commission
study done years ago estimated that a meltdown in the U.S. could injure
73,000 and kill 27,000, while causing $17 billion in property damage.

The so-called "inherently safe" reactors that have been proposed may be
feasible to build decades from now, but even they are untenable because we
will still have no means of safely disposing of the spent fuel they will
generate.

Such waste already presents serious problems. Since it stays dangerously
radioactive for fifty thousand years and cannot be safely disposed of, voters
who don't want it near them defeat dump-site proposals. As a result, the

waste is temporarily stored. By the year 2001 we may have seventy-two thousand tons of it in the United States. And by that time we will also have enough low-level milling and mining waste to build a mound as high as a man's head from New York to Los Angeles.

If waste from fission reactors is dangerous, building the nuclear weapons they make possible is insane. As Carl Sagan and others have pointed out, a nuclear conflict cannot be won because in addition to releasing deadly radiation, it would result in a "nuclear winter."

The nuclear weapons industry has already wreaked havoc on public health. According to the U.S. Department of Energy, American laboratories and plants that make nuclear weapons have released radioactive isotopes on at least 155 occasions (no one knows how many instances have not been reported). This pollution has probably caused thousands of cancers and birth defects in humans and an incalculable amount of damage to wildlife, and Congress has estimated that it will cost up to $200 billion over the next hundred years to clean it up. Nuclear weapons testing is credited with even greater damage. According to Dr. John Gofman, atomic testing has probably already condemned 1,116,000 people to developing lung cancer. Ironically, our nuclear weapons may already be obsolete; the threat of Soviet aggression, which they were designed to deter, seems to have disintegrated.

Let's not wait until tens of thousands of Americans are killed by a meltdown or tens of millions by a nuclear war triggered by some software or hardware malfunction. Let's put a stop to nuclear power now. Let's begin right here at home by making nuclear power and nuclear waste illegal in our community.

Thank you for your consideration.

Sincerely,

—
—
—
—

—

—

—

—

RE: Establishing hazardous waste facilities

Dear

I believe it is imperative that a permanent facility for collecting and properly disposing of hazardous wastes be established in our county.

The amount of hazardous waste generated by Americans every year amounts to more than two thousand pounds per person. Much of it is disposed of in ordinary landfills. Up to a quarter of it consists of household wastes like batteries containing lead, cadmium, and/or mercury (about ten per person each year), paint and paint products containing heavy metals and solvents, mothballs, oven cleaners, explosives, insecticides, herbicides, rodenticides, fungicides, flammables, acids, drain cleaners, furniture polish and strippers, motor oil, even radioactive smoke detectors. And since EPA regulations allow industries that generate less than one hundred kilograms of hazardous waste per month to dispose of their wastes in landfills as well, they often include highly toxic, flammable, corrosive, and/or explosive industrial chemicals as well.

Much of what does not go to landfills is poured into sewers. This includes an estimated average of ten ounces of recyclable motor oil (enough to spoil seventy-eight thousand gallons of drinking water) for every man, woman, and child each year, and an unknown quantity of antifreeze, flammable solvents, insecticides, rat poisons, etc. Still more of it is simply dumped on the ground in places where it endangers water supplies.

Landfills are not built to handle hazardous materials. Neither are sewer systems. And neither are highway verges, mine shafts, vacant lots, or streams. Inevitably, hazardous wastes disposed of in these places harm wildlife, and eventually contaminate the soil and aquifers that are the sources of our own food and water supplies. And once these are contaminated, they may remain unusable for decades or centuries.

But until permanent, convenient facilities are set up to allow for the proper disposal of hazardous waste, people will continue this unnecessary polluting, and our own health and the health of our environment will suffer the ever-worsening cumulative effects—including cancer, birth defects, and genetic damage.

I urge you to help protect our environment and the health of the people in our community by working with county officials to establish permanent, convenient, safe hazardous-waste collection and disposal facilities.

Thank you for your consideration.

Sincerely,

—
—
—
—

—
—
—
—

RE: Planting more trees in our community

Dear

I am writing today to ask you to support and encourage the volunteer planting of more trees along our streets, on the grounds of our official buildings, and elsewhere in our community.

Trees are vital to the health of the biosphere. They prevent a runaway greenhouse effect by absorbing carbon dioxide, stabilize soil, provide humidification and evaporative cooling (as much as ten degrees in urban areas), and emit the major portion of the oxygen we breathe. They also give us food, wood, shade, and beauty, and they shelter the majority of the Earth's plant, animal, and insect species.

Unfortunately, we have been cutting trees down at an escalating rate for so many centuries that we now stand on the brink of environmental catastrophe. We are razing the 70 million-year-old tropical rain forests that produce 40 percent of the oxygen in the air at the rate of 51 acres per minute, and are leaving behind eroding deserts. Our rain forests may all be gone by the year 2032. About 87 percent of the original ancient forests in the northwestern U.S. are already gone. Canada cuts 247,000 more acres of trees than it replants every year. And all over the world trees are constantly being bulldozed for farms, buildings, highways, and parking lots, and never replaced.

This deforestation is one of the reasons carbon dioxide, which traps solar heat and creates a greenhouse effect, has reached such a high concentration in our atmosphere that global warming has begun. Global average temperatures are already about half a degree higher than they were a century ago, and they could rise by as much as nine degrees in the next few decades, melting the Earth's ice caps, flooding coastal areas, turning farmland into deserts, and spawning frequent, violent storms.

This greenhouse effect is progressive. Even if we stop burning gasoline and coal to prevent more carbon dioxide from building up in the atmosphere, global warming will continue for years unless we do something to remove the carbon dioxide already in the air—something like planting more trees.

Were we able to grow enough trees, we could stabilize our atmosphere and bring global warming to a halt, buying ourselves some time to develop alternative fuels. Of course a project of that magnitude is far beyond the ability of any community or even any nation. But every tree planted, regardless of its location, helps reduce the level of carbon dioxide in the air a little bit, thereby slowing the greenhouse effect.

Grassroots tree-planting projects have already begun all over the world. The American Forestry Association's Global Releaf program, for instance, which began on Arbor Day, 1989, is helping Americans plant 100 million trees by 1992. But more government involvement is needed. Every local government needs to pitch in and do its share by including more trees in official building projects, aiding volunteer efforts at reforestation and education, publicly endorsing tree planting, and sponsoring tree plantings by individual volunteers and organizations like the Boy Scouts of America.

Please join those of us who support reforestation by publicly endorsing it, and by working to see that seedlings and guidelines are provided to any individual or group wishing to plant trees in our community.

Thank you for your consideration.

Sincerely,

—
—
—
—

Appendix A

Source List

Below is a list of sources of information and products that may prove helpful to those who want to help save the environment. It is by no means a complete catalog, but is simply a compilation of data accumulated during background research for *Dear Mr. President.* Any omissions of important sources of information are strictly unintentional.

Inclusion in this appendix does not constitute endorsement by the author. And remember, names can be misleading; the "Council of Energy Awareness," for instance, is actually a lobby for the nuclear power industry. So before you decide to join or contribute to an organization, make sure you know what it represents.

Also, there can be no guarantee that all the addresses and telephone numbers given are accurate. Many environmental organizations and manufacturers and retailers of environmentally benign products are new. Some operate on shoestring budgets and thus are obliged to change locations often because of overhead costs and other considerations. Others are growing so fast they must continually move to larger facilities. If you are not sure, adding the words "Address correction requested" a quarter-inch below your return address will get your letter returned to you with a corrected address in the event an addressee has moved. (This can be especially helpful, since the post office only forwards first class mail for one year.)

Several volumes would be required to explain what many of the organizations listed have done and are doing, what they publish, and so on. The short remarks that follow many of the entries in this list are not intended to substitute for such an explanation; they merely point out an item or two that readers may find particularly useful or interesting.

Sources:

20/20 Vision
30 Cottage St.
Amherst, MA 01002
(800) 669–1782 or (413) 549–4555

A network of individuals who take twenty minutes each month to communicate with policy makers on peace and on the environment. Issues a report of the results twice each year. $20 annual membership fee.

Abundant Life Seed Foundation
P.O. Box 772
Port Townsend, WA 98368
(206) 385–5660

A source of tree seeds that have not been hybridized, treated with pesticides, or radiated.

Acid Rain Foundation
1410 Varsity Dr.
Raleigh, NC 27606
(919) 828–9443

Acid Rain Precipitation Data Base
New York State Department of the Environment
50 Wolf Rd.
Albany, NY 12233
(518) 474–2121

African Wildlife Foundation
1717 Massachusetts Ave., NW, Suite 602
Washington, DC 20036
(800) 344–8875

Seeks to preserve biological diversity.

Ag Access
603 4th St.
Davis, CA 95616
(916) 756–7177

Sells book on composting titled *Let It Rot* (152 pages).

Air Pollution Control Association
P.O. Box 2861
Pittsburgh, PA 15230
(412) 232–3444

Alaska Conservation Foundation
430 W. 7th Ave., Suite 215
Anchorage, AK 99501
(907) 276–1917

Coordinates thirty organizations that are trying to protect Alaskan land and waters.

Alcoa Recycling Company, Inc.
1501 Alcoa Building
Pittsburg, PA 15219
(412) 777–1580

Gives advice on where and how to recycle aluminum. Publishes a guide and list of regional contacts on starting can collection and full-scale recycling centers. A video showing can recycling is available to communities and schools.

Alliance to Save Energy
1725 K St., NW
Washington, DC 20036
(202) 857–0666

Alpha Solarco
11534 Gondola Dr.
Cincinnati, OH 45241
(513) 771–1690

Manufactures photovoltaic equipment.

Aluminum Recycling Association
1000 16th St., NW, Suite 603
Washington, DC 20036
(202) 785–0951

The American Council for an Energy-Efficient Economy
1001 Connecticut Ave., NW, Suite 535
Washington, DC 20036
(202) 429–8873

Sells *Saving Energy and Money with Home Appliances* ($2) and *The Most Energy Efficient Appliances*.

American Forestry Association
Global Releaf Program
P.O. Box 2000
Washington, DC 20013
(800) 368–5748 or (202) 667–3300

Wants to help Americans plant 100 million trees by 1992.

American Recycling Market
Recycled Products Guide
P.O. Box 577
Ogdensburg, NY 13669
(800) 267–0707

Ask about their directory, *Recycled Products Guide*, and their computer data base.

American Solar Energy Society
2400 Central Ave., Unit B–1
Boulder, CO 80301
(303) 443–3130

American Soybean Association
P.O. Box 419200
St. Louis, MO 63141
(800) 688–7692

Ask about soy-based printing inks.

American Wind Energy Associations
777 North Capital St., NE
Washington, DC 20005
(202) 408–8988

Americans for Safe Food
1875 Connecticut Ave., NW, Suite 300
Washington, DC 20009-5728
(202) 332–9110

The Amicus Journal
Natural Resources Defense Council
40 N. 20th St.
New York, NY 10011
(212) 727–2700

Quarterly magazine covering thoughts and opinions on national and international environmental policies and actions.

Antarctica Project
707 D St., SE
Washington, DC 20003
(202) 544–0236

Association of Community Associations for Reform Now (ACORN)
739 8th St., SE
Washington, DC 20003
(202) 547–9292

Concerned with toxics, health, taxes, community improvement.

Audubon, The Magazine of the National Audubon Society
950 Third Ave.
New York, NY 10022
(212) 832–3200

Bimonthly magazine dedicated to protecting wildlife, natural resources, and the environment.

Baby Bunz and Company
P.O. Box 1717
Sebastopol, CA 95473
(707) 829–5347

Sells natural-fiber diaper products, etc. Catalog ($1).

Balloons and Clowns
703 N. Milwaukee Ave.
Libertyville, IL 60048
(708) 680–3224

Provides information on the effects of helium-filled balloons on the environment. Send stamped, self-addressed envelope.

Bergey Windpower
2001 Priestley Ave.
Norman, OK 73069
(405) 364–4212

Manufactures wind-energy equipment.

Bio-Bottoms
P.O. Box 6009
617C Second St.
Petaluma, CA 94953
(707) 778–7945

Sells natural-fiber diaper products, etc. Catalog ($1).

Bio Cycle
J G Press
419 State Ave.
Emmaus, PA 18049
(215) 967–4135

A monthly magazine aimed at municipal solid waste and sludge ($58/year). J G Press also sells *The Biocycle Guide to the Art and Science of Composting.*

The Bio-Integral Resource Center (BIRC)
P.O. Box 7414
Berkeley, CA 94707
(510) 524–2567

Offers a publication: *Least Toxic Pet Management for Fleas.* Also publishes *IPM Practitioner* (magazine), which deals with integral pest management.

The Body Shop
485 Madison Ave.
New York, NY 10022
(212) 832–0812

Sells body products that are not tested on animals and are environmentally safe.

Buzzworm, The Environmental Journal
2305 Canyon Blvd., Suite 206
Boulder, CO 80302
(303) 442–1969

Bimonthly magazine.

Catalyst
P.O. Box 1308
Montpelier, VT 05601
(802) 223–7943

Provides workshops, networking, etc., for those who want to save rain forests. Publishes a quarterly newsletter, *Catalyst*, which promotes investment for social change.

Center for Environmental Education
1725 DeSales St., NW
Washington, DC 20036
(202) 429–5609

Publishes reference books on oceans. Fights against the illegal trading of wildlife and pushes for marine conservation.

Center for Environmental Information and Acid Rain Information Clearinghouse
46 Prince St.
Rochester, NY 14607
(716) 271–3550

Center for Marine Conservation
1725 DeSales St., NW
Washington, DC 20036
(202) 429–5609

Sponsors a nationwide beach cleanup every September 23.

Center for Plastics Recycling Research
Rutgers, The State University of New Jersey
Busch Campus, Building 3529
P.O. Box 1179
Piscataway, NJ 08855–1179
(908) 932–4402

Center for Science in the Public Interest
1875 Connecticut Ave., NW, Suite 300
Washington, DC 20009–5728
(202) 332–9110

Center for the Biology of Natural Systems (CBNS)
Queens College
Flushing, NY 11367
(718) 670–4180

Researches environmental subjects like renewable energy and disposal of municipal solid waste.

Citizen's Clearinghouse for Hazardous Waste
P.O. Box 6806
Falls Church, VA 22040
(703) 276–7070

Assists grassroots and environmental action groups. Publishes a newsletter, *Everyone's Backyard* ($25/year, 4 issues).

Citizens for a Better Environment (CBE)
407 South Dearborn, Suite 1775
Chicago, IL 60605
(312) 939–1530

City of Berkeley, California
Precycling Information
(510) 644–6858

A source of information for communities wishing to institute precycling (choosing products that can be recycled).

Clean Water Action Project
1320 18th St., NW
Washington, DC 20036
(202) 457–1286

Provides information and organizing assistance to groups trying to clean up the environment, and strategy to groups publicizing electoral candidates' positions on environmental issues.

Climate Institute
316 Pennsylvania Ave., SE
Washington, DC 20003
(202) 547–0104

Tries to help the public understand global warming and prevent ozone depletion. Publishes *Climate Alert*, a quarterly newsletter.

Clothcrafters, Inc.
P.O. Box 176
Elkhart Lake, WI 53020
(414) 876–2112

Sells cloth shower curtains, coffee filters, tote bags, cheesecloth bags, etc.

Committee for Nuclear Responsibility
P.O. Box 421993
San Francisco, CA 94142
(415) 776–8299

Concerned with radiation dangers, even those posed by medical procedures.

The Committee for Sustainable Agriculture (CSA)
P.O. Box 1300
Colfax, CA 95713
(916) 346–2777

Sponsors educational programs and conferences and publishes *Organic Food Matters* each quarter.

CONCERN, Inc.
1794 Columbia Rd., NW
Washington, DC 20009
(202) 328–8160

Source for *Waste: Choices for Communities*, a thirty-page booklet on waste-disposal options and their impacts and new methods of sound waste management.

Conservation Foundation, Inc.
1250 24th St., NW, Suite 500
Washington, DC 20037–1175
(202) 293–4800

Researches management of resources and the environment and publishes a newsletter, *Resolve*.

Conservatree Paper Company
10 Lombard St., Suite 250
San Francisco, CA 94111
(800) 522–9200; in California (415) 433–1000

Sells recycled office paper in quantity.

Consumer Product Safety Commission (CPSC)
5401 Westbard Ave.
Bethesda, MD 20207
(800) 638–2772 or (301) 492–6800

Container Recycling Institute
710 G St., SE
Washington, DC 20003
(202) 543–9449

Co-op America
2100 M St., NW, Suite 403
Washington, DC 20063
(202) 872–5307

Works to promote responsibility, self-reliance, co-operation, and a healthier environment.

Cornell University
Audio-Visual Center
8 Business and Technology Park
Ithaca, NY 14850
(607) 255–2091

Source for a list of slide shows, videos, and written educational aids for youth concerning solid waste.

Cousteau Society
930 W. 21st St.
Norfolk, VA 23517
(804) 627–1144

Pioneered many aspects of underwater research in the oceans, the Amazon, Antarctica, etc., and informed the public through its TV programs. Has about 300,000 members.

Creating Our Future
1640 Francisco St.
Berkeley, CA 94703
(510) 841–3020

Supplies an information packet made up by high-school students and titled *How to Organize a Rainforest Awareness Week at Your School*.

Defenders of Wildlife
1244 19th St., NW
Washington, DC 20036–2416
(202) 659–9510

Ask for their booklet, *Deadly Throwaways*, about
the effects of litter on the environment. They try to
preserve native species and restore threatened species and habitat. Their magazine, *Defenders*, is
available for a membership fee (6 issues/year).

Delaware Solid Waste Authority
P.O. Box 455
Dover, DE 19903

Source for "Trash Can Dan" coloring books that
help children learn about trash and the recycling
process.

Department of Energy (DOE)
1000 Independence Ave., SW
Washington, DC 20285–0001
(202) 586–5000

- Conservation and Renewable Energy Inquiry
  and Referral Service (CAREIRS)
  P.O. Box 8900
  Silver Spring, MD 20907
  (800) 523–2929

- National Appropriate Technology Service
  (NATS)
  P.O. Box 2525
  Butte, MT 59702–2525
  (800) 428–2525; in Montana (800) 428–1718

- National Center for Appropriate Technology
  (NCAT)
  3040 Continental Dr.
  P.O. Box 3838
  Butte, MT 59701
  (406) 494–4572

- Office of Conservation and Renewable Energy
  1000 Independence Ave., SW
  Washington, DC 20585
  (202) 586–9220

- Solar Energy Research Institute
  1617 Cole Blvd.
  Golden, CO 80401
  (303) 231–1000

Department of Health and Human Services
Hazard Evaluations and Technical Assistance
Branch
Division of Surveillance
Hazard Evaluation and Field Studies
5555 Ridge Ave, Columbia Township
Cincinnati, OH 45226
(513) 841–4428

Diaperaps
P.O. Box 3050
Granada Hills, CA 91394
(800) 251–4321 for orders or (800) 477–3424 for
customer service

Sells cotton and nylon diaper covers.

Earth Care Paper Company
P.O. Box 7070
Madison, WI 53707–7070
(608) 277–2900

Sells recycled office paper, greeting cards, and
wrapping paper, cellulose sandwich bags, etc. Ask
for their free catalog.

Earth First!
305 N. 6th St.
Madison, WI 53704
(608) 241–9426

Promotes the defense of natural diversity by
organizing media "road shows" and direct-action
task forces.

Earth Island Institute
300 Broadway, Suite 28
San Francisco, CA 94133
(415) 788–3666

Will tell you what can be done about endangered
species. Ask for information about saving dolphins
from tuna nets and about the Climate Protection
Network and Environmental Litigation Fund. EII
promotes appropriate technology.

Ecco Bella
6 Provost Square, Suite 602
Caldwell, NJ 07006
(201) 226–5799

Sells biodegradable cellulose bags in quantity and in custom sizes. Also sells recycled paper products, biodegradable soaps, body products, household products, etc.

Eco-Cycle
P.O. Box 4193
Boulder, CO 80306
(303) 444–6634

Source for an information packet about establishing a recycling collection program using volunteers ($15).

Ecological Engineering Associates
13 Marconi Lane
Marion, MA 02738
(508) 748–3224

Sells and consults on solar-aquatic waste-disposal systems.

Ecological Water Products, Inc.
266 Main St., Suite 18
Medfield, MA 02052
(508) 359–5001

Sells low-flow shower heads, faucet aerators, toilet dams, etc.

The Ecology Center
2530 San Pablo Avenue
Berkeley, CA 94702
(510 548–2220

Source of information on "stamping out" polystyrene foam and on curbside recycling. Also, ask for their fact sheet on detergents (and phosphates).

Energy Conversion Devices/Sovonics Solar Systems
1675 W. Maple Rd.
Troy, MI 48084–7197
(313) 280–1900

Manufactures photovoltaic equipment.

Environment
Heldref Publications
4000 Albemarle St., NW
Washington, DC 20016
(800) 365–9753

Magazine containing scientific material on the environment and the effects of technology on society. Subscriptions are $24/year for 10 issues.

Environmental Action
1525 New Hampshire Ave., NW
Washington, DC 20036
(202) 745–4870

Bimonthly magazine of environmental news, issues, and policy for a general audience.

Environmental Action Coalition
625 Broadway
New York, NY 10012
(212) 677–1601

Ask for information on how batteries pollute the environment.

Environmental Action Foundation
1525 New Hampshire Ave., NW
Washington, DC 20036
(202) 745–4871

Ask for the *"Bottle Bills" Solid Waste Fact Sheet* from their Solid Waste Alternatives Project and for information on their Energy Conservation Coalition. Publishes *Environmental Action*.

Environmental Defense Fund
257 Park Avenue South, 16th Floor
New York, NY 10010
(800) 225–5333 or (212) 505–2100

Ask for their free brochure on recycling and information on recycling in your area. EDF has been instrumental in fighting the greenhouse effect. It has 100,000 members.

Environmental Hazards Management Institute (EHMI)
10 Newmarket Rd.
P.O. Box 70
Durham, NH 03824
(603) 868–1496 or (800) 446–5256

Sells *Household Hazardous Waste Wheel* ($3.75). Provides information on innovative environmental programs and educational products on waste management.

Environmental Law Institute
1616 P St., NW, 2nd Floor
Washington, DC 20036–1493
(202) 939–3800

Does research and lobbying, and handles litigation involving compensation for victims of toxic materials.

Environmental Policy Institute
218 D St., SE
Washington, DC 20003–1900
(202) 544–2600

Environmental Protection Agency (EPA)
401 M St., SW
Washington, DC 20460–0001
(202) 260–7751

- Asbestos Hotline (202) 554–1404

- Emergency Planning and Community Right-to-know (800) 535–0202

- Inspector General's Whistle Blower Hotline (800) 424–4000; in Washington, DC, (202) 382–4977

- National Pesticides Telecommunications Network (800) 858–7378; in Texas, (806) 743–3091, twenty-four hours a day

- Office of Air and Radiation (202) 382–5580

- Office of Drinking Water Criteria and Standards (202) 382–5543

- Office of Emergency and Remedial Response (202) 382–2180

- Office of Hazardous Waste (202) 475–9810

- Office of Radiation Programs (202) 475–9600

- Office of Solid Waste (202) 382–4627

- Office of Toxic Substances and Toxic Substances Control Act (TSCA) Assistance Information Service (202) 554–1404

- Public Information Center (202) 382–2080

- Radon Action Programs (202) 475–9605

- RCRA/Superfund Hotline and Solid Waste Hotline (800) 424–9346; in Washington, DC, (202) 382–3000

- Safe Drinking Water Hotline (800) 426–4791; in Washington, DC, (202) 382–5533

- Small Business Hotline (202) 557–7777

FSC Paper Corp.
13101 Pulaski Rd.
Alsip, IL 60658–2008
(708) 389–8520

A supplier of 100 percent recycled newsprint.

Fafco, Inc.
2690 Middlefield Rd.
Redwood City, CA 94063
(510) 363–2690

Manufactures solar-thermal equipment.

Florida Solar Energy Center
300 State Road 401
Cape Canaveral, FL 32920–4099
(407) 783–0300

Food and Water
Box 770
Blairstown, NJ 07825
(908) 362–8800

Ask about anti-irradiation groups in your area.

Friends of the Earth
218 D St., SE
Washington, DC 20003–1900
(202) 544–2600

Concentrates on toxic waste, ozone layer, conservation, pesticides, etc. Publishes a quarterly newsletter for members. Will tell you what you can do to help the environment, endangered species, and water pollution.

Friends of the Trees
P.O. Box 1466
Chelan, WA 98816

Promotes worldwide reforestation. Distributes seeds, information on plants, etc. Publishes the *International Green Front Report*.

GIE Publishing
4012 Bridge Ave.
Cleveland, OH 44113
(800) 456–0707

Sources for recycled paper can be found in their *Paper Stock Dealers Directory* ($25 + $2.50 postage & handling).

Garbage
P.O. Box 56519
Boulder, CO 80322
(800) 274–9909

An environmental magazine dealing with all aspects of practical ecology.

Geothermal Resources Council
P.O. Box 1350
Davis, CA 95617–1350
(916) 758–2360

Glass Packaging Institute
1801 K St., NW, Suite 1105L
Washington, DC 20006–1301
(202) 887–4850

Provides free pamphlets concerning glass recycling.

Greenhouse Crisis Foundation
1130 17th St., NW, Suite 630
Washington, DC 20036
(202) 466–2823

Working on many aspects of studying and combating global warming.

Greenpeace Toxic Campaign
1017 W. Jackson Blvd.
Chicago, IL 60607
(312) 666–3305

Ask for *A Citizen's Toxic Waste Audit Manual* ($5 donation requested).

Greenpeace USA
1436 U St., NW
Washington, DC 20009
(202) 462–1177

A major international organization embracing a wide scope of environmental issues. Known for direct action, even radical activism. Has 2.7 million members worldwide.

The Greens
Clearinghouse
Box 30208
Kansas City, MO 64112
(816) 931–9366

A clearinghouse for people interested in the Green movement that has become influential in Australia, Austria, Belgium, Sweden, and West Germany.

HearthSong
P.O. Box B
Sebastopol, CA 95473–0601
(800) 325–2502

Ask for their free catalog of toys, games, books, art materials, etc., that are not made of plastic and do not need batteries.

Home Energy
2124 Kittredge St., no. 95
Berkeley, CA 94704
(510) 524–5405

Publishes *Consumer Guide to Energy-Saving Lights* ($2).

The Household Hazardous Waste Project
1031 E. Battlefield, Suite 214
Springfield, MO 65807
(417) 889–5000

Ask for *The Guide to Hazardous Products Around the Home* (recipes for alternatives to toxic household substances, tested by Southwest Missouri State University—$9.95).

INFORM
381 Park Ave. South
New York, NY 10016
(212) 689–4040

Researches environmental subjects like pollution, toxic waste, garbage, etc.

Institute for Alternative Agriculture
9200 Edmonton Rd.
Greenbelt, MD 20770
(301) 441–8777

Institute for Local Self-Reliance
2425 18th St., NW
Washington, DC 20009
(202) 232–4108

Information for communities on technical aspects and economics of solid waste, and a guide to recycling strategies are available.

Institute of Scrap Recycling Industries
1627 K St., NW, Suite 700
Washington, DC 20006–1795
(202) 466–4050

This trade association is a source for *Scrap* magazine and other publications.

Interbath, Inc.
427 N. Baldwin Park Blvd.
City of Industry, CA 91746
(800) 423–9485 or (818) 369–1841

Sells low-flow shower heads.

International Alliance for Sustainable Agriculture
1701 University Ave., SE
Minneapolis, MN 55414
(612) 331–1099

International Wildlife
National Wildlife Federation
8925 Leesburg Pike
Vienna, VA 22184
(800) 345–4060

Bimonthly magazine covering wildlife and environmental problems caused by human interaction with nature.

Izaak Walton League of America
1401 Wilson Blvd., Level B
Arlington, VA 22209–2318
(703) 528–1818

Distributes free *Save Our Streams* booklet and other information.

Keep America Beautiful, Inc.
9 W. Broad St.
Stamford, CT 06902
(203) 323–8987

The Learning Alliance
494 Broadway
New York, NY 10012
(212) 226–7171

Provides effective strategies for people wishing to take action on environmental issues.

Livos Plantchemistry
1365 Rufina Circle
Santa Fe, NM 87501
(800) 621–2591

Source for nontoxic and natural cleaners, waxes, stains, paints, and finishes.

Luz International
924 Westwood Blvd., Suite 1000
Los Angeles, CA 90024
(213) 208–7444

Builds solar-thermal plants.

Materials World Publishing
6082 Ralston Ave.
Richmond, CA 94805
(510) 232–7724

Publishes *The Lone Recycler*, a comic book for kids about changing waste into resources ($3 + $1 postage & handling).

Mothers and Others For Pesticide Limits
Natural Resources Defense Council
1350 New York Ave., NW, Suite 300
Washington, DC 20005
(202) 783–7800

Source for information on pesticides, including a newsletter titled *tlc* and a book titled *For Our Kids' Sake* ($7.95).

Murdock Health Care
10 Mountain Springs Pkwy.
Springville, UT 84663
(800) 926–8883 or (801) 489–3635

Supplies organic herbs, etc., and sends a free information packet helpful in discontinuing the use of polystyrene foam.

National Association for Plastic Container Recycling (NAPCoR)
4878 Parkway Plaza Blvd., Suite 260
Charlotte, NC 28217
(704) 357–3250

Helps plastic recycling projects get a start and promotes voluntary recycling of plastic soda bottles.

National Association of Diaper Services
2017 Walnut St.
Philadelphia, PA 19103
(215) 569–3650

Provides information on where to find services that supply reusable cloth diapers.

National Association of Solvent Recyclers
1333 New Hampshire Ave., NW, Suite 1100
Washington, DC 20036
(202) 463–6956

Ask who recycles solvents in your area.

National Association of Towns and Townships
1522 K St., NW
Washington, DC 20005
(202) 737–5200

Ask about *Why Waste a Second Chance: A Small Town Guide to Recycling.*

National Audubon Society
950 3rd Ave.
New York, NY 10022–2793
(212) 832–3200

Provides information on protecting wildlife, etc. A conservative group of 550,000 members that has been in operation for eighty-five years. It operates one-quarter million acres of wildlife sanctuaries and does lobbying on energy policy, etc. Publishes *Audubon.*

National Center for Environmental Health Strategies
1100 Rural Ave.
Voorhees, NJ 08043
(609) 429–5358

Puts out a quarterly newsletter, *The Delicate Balance*, and a report on sensitivity to chemicals.

National Center for Policy Alternatives
1875 Connecticut Ave., NW, Suite 710
Washington, DC 20009
(202) 387–6030

National Coalition Against the Misuse of Pesticides (NCAMP)
701 E St., SE, Suite 200
Washington, DC 20003
(202) 543–5450

Provides information on the dangers of pesticide use and how to stop it. Puts out a newsletter: *Pesticides and You.*

National Parks
1015 31st St., NW
Washington, DC 20007
(202) 944–8530

Bimonthly magazine dedicated to preserving national parks, wildlife habitats, and natural areas. Written for the highly educated reader.

National Recycling Coalition
1101 30th St., NW, Suite 305
Washington, DC 20007
(202) 625–6406

Made up of individuals, industrial groups, environmental groups, and state and local governments. Members get a quarterly newsletter and discounts on the National Recycling Congress, *Resource Recycling*, and the hiring of some speakers.

National Toxics Campaign Fund
1168 Commonwealth Ave.
Boston, MA 02134
(617) 232–0327 or (617) 232–4014

Orchestrates and supports grassroots groups fighting against toxic pollution and tries to prevent more of such pollution. Publishes a newsletter, *Toxic Times*, for members. Has fifteen offices across the country.

National Wildlife
8925 Leesburg Pike
Vienna, VA 22184–0001
(703) 790–4000

Bimonthly magazine on wildlife and the environment. Published by the National Wildlife Federation.

National Wildlife Federation
1400 16th St., NW
Washington, DC 20036–2266
(800) 432–6564 or (202) 797–6800

Involved in protecting wildlife. Ask about their Backyard Wildlife Habitat Program. This organization has nearly 6 million supporters, so it is respected by politicians. Publishes *National Wildlife, International Wildlife,* and a number of other publications.

Native Forest Action Council
P.O. Box 2171
Eugene, OR 97402
(503) 688–2600

Working to protect old-growth forests in the U.S.

Native Seed Foundation
Star Route
Moyie Springs, ID 83845
(208) 267–7938

A source for tree seeds that have not been hybridized, treated with pesticides, or radiated.

Natural Resources Defense Council (NRDC)
40 W. 20th St.
New York, NY 10011
(212) 727–2700

Distributes a pamphlet: *Saving the Ozone Layer: A Citizen Action Guide.* Is starting a kids' environmental organization. NRDC has 170,000 members. Ask about nuclear safety, water pollution, etc. Publishes *The Amicus Journal.*

Nature Conservancy International
1815 Lynn St.
Arlington, VA 22209–2016
(703) 841–5300

Works with private landowners to preserve lands all over the world. Has 590,000 members.

North Carolina Solar Center
Box 7401
NC State University
Raleigh, NC 27695–7401
(919) 515–3480

Northeast Sustainable Energy Association
23 Ames St.
Greenfield, MA 01301
(413) 774–6051

Northern Arizona Wind & Sun
2725 E. Lakin Dr., no. 2
Flagstaff, AZ 86004
(602) 526–8017

Distributes solar-electric products.

Northern Power Systems
1 North Wind Rd.
Moretown, VT 05660
(802) 496–2955

Manufactures wind-energy equipment.

Northwest Coalition for Alternatives to Pesticides
(NCAP)
P.O. Box 1393
Eugene, OR 97440
(503) 344–5044

Nuclear Information and Resource Service (NIRS)
1424 16th St., NW, Suite 601
Washington, DC 20036
(202) 328–0002

A source of information for antinuclear and safe-energy activists. Has brought suits to overturn rules and force the release of documents. Has a computer bulletin board, NIRSNET, that can provide information on every U.S. nuclear plant. Ask about renewable energy.

Nuclear Regulatory Commission (NRC)
1717 H St., NW
Washington, DC 20555

Occupational Safety and Health Administration
(OSHA)
Department of Labor
200 Constitution Ave., NW, Room N3647
Washington, DC 20210–0001
(202) 523–8148

Organic Foods Production Association of North America
P.O. Box 1078
Greenfield, MA 01301
(413) 774–7511

A marketing network of farmers, processors, and distributors of organic foods that stores can contact to find suppliers for authentic, quality organic food.

Organic Gardening
Rodale Press, Inc.
33 E. Minor St.
Emmaus, PA 18098
(215) 967–5171

Magazine published nine times per year.

P3, The Earth-Based Magazine for Kids
P.O. Box 52
Montgomery, VT 05470
(802) 326–4669

Environmental magazine. Subscriptions are $12.

Paper Recycling Committee
American Paper Institute
260 Madison Ave.
New York, NY 10016–2439
(212) 340–0600

Provides free pamphlets on recycling paper.

Pennsylvania Resources Council
P.O. Box 88
Media, PA 19063
(215) 565–9131

Provides a booklet titled *The Environmental Shopper* and a list of products packaged in recycled materials.

Pesticides Action Network
965 Mission St., no. 514
San Francisco, CA 94103
(415) 541–9140

An international coalition of people and organizations against the misuse of pesticides.

Photocomm, Inc.
930 Idaho Maryland Rd.
Grass Valley, CA 95945
(800) 544–6466

Sells solar modules and related hardware. Catalog available ($2).

Planet Drum Foundation
Box 31251
San Francisco, CA 94131
(415) 285–6556

A coalition of sixty North American groups advocating saving the Earth by restoring your own region. Publishes *Raise the Stakes* newspaper.

Power Kinetics, Inc.
415 River St.
Troy, NY 12180
(518) 271-0782

Manufactures solar-thermal equipment.

Project Rose (Recycled Oil Saves Energy)
P.O. Box 870203
Tuscaloosa, AL 35487-0203
(205) 348-4878

Provides information on recycling oil.

Public Citizens Critical Mass Energy Project
215 Pennsylvania Ave., SE
Washington, DC 20003
(202) 546-4996

Founded by Ralph Nader. Tries to close down nuclear reactors and proposes nonpolluting, safe alternatives. Has been involved in numerous litigations. Publishes *Nuclear Lemons*, the *National Directory of Safe Energy Organizations*, etc.

Public Information Office
Massachusetts Audubon Society
South Great Road
Lincoln, MA 01773
(617) 259-9500

Source for booklets: *Heating Systems, How to Weatherize Your Home or Apartment, All About Insulation*.

Publication Dept.
Local Government Commission
909 12th St., Suite 205
Sacramento, CA 95814
(916) 448-1198

Sells *Making the Switch: Alternatives to Using Toxic Chemicals in the Home* ($6).

Radioactive Waste Campaign
118 N. 11th St.
Brooklyn, NY 10211
(718) 387-8786

Rainforest Action Network
301 Broadway, Suite A
San Francisco, CA 94133
(415) 398-4404

Ask for information on what you can do to help stop deforestation. Publishes the *World Rainforest Report* each quarter.

Rainforest Alliance
270 Lafayette St., no. 512
New York, NY 10012
(212) 941-1900

Real Goods Trading Corporation
966 Mazzoni St.
Ukiah, CA 95482
(800) 762-7325

Ask for their eighty-page catalog of every conceivable alternative product from wind generators to composting toilets.

Recycling Today
4012 Bridge Ave.
Cleveland, OH 44113
(216) 961-4130

A monthly magazine focusing on recycling technology and industrial issues.

Renew America
1400 16th St., NW, Suite 710
Washington, DC 20036
(202) 232-2252

Send them your stories about people in your community who are working to save the planet. A $25 membership gets you a quarterly newsletter and other information on energy and the environment. Ask about the *State of the States* report.

Renewable Fuels Association
1 Massachusetts Ave., NW, Suite 820
Washington, DC 20001
(800) 542-3835 or (202) 289-3835

Resource Recycling
P.O. Box 10540
Portland, OR 97210
(800) 227–1424 or (503) 227–1319

A monthly magazine aimed at residential and commercial waste ($42/year).

Rising Sun Enterprises
P.O. Box 1728
Basalt, CO 81621
(303) 927–8051

Sells energy-efficient light bulbs. Catalog/consumer guide available ($5).

Rockline, Inc.
1113 Maryland Ave.
P.O. Box 1007
Sheboygan, WI 53082–1007
(414) 459–4160

Ask them about unbleached coffee filters.

Rocky Mountain Institute
1739 Snowmass Creek Rd.
Snowmass, CO 81654–9199
(303) 927–3851

A think tank concerned with renewable energy resources and more efficient use of energy. Publishes special reports and the *RMI Newsletter*.

Rural Community Assistance Program (RCAP)
602 S. King St.
Leesburg, VA 22075
(703) 478–8652

Concerned with water quality.

San Francisco Recycling Program
271 City Hall
San Francisco, CA 94102

Ask for their booklet: *Your Office Paper Recycling Guide*.

Save A Tree
P.O. Box 862
Berkeley, CA 94701
(510) 843–5233

Sells reusable canvas shopping bags ($9).

Seattle Tilth Association
4649 Sunnyside N.
Seattle, WA 98103
(206) 633–0451

Supplies a brochure: *Home Composting* ($2—send stamped, self-addressed envelope with $0.50 postage).

Seventh Generation
Colchester, VT 05446–1672
(800) 456–1177

Sells 150 conservation and recycled products including low-flow shower heads, string grocery bags, cleaners, toilet tissue, books.

Sierra
730 Polk St.
San Francisco, CA 94109
(415) 776–2211

Bimonthly magazine covering conservation, environmental politics, etc. Aimed at well-educated readers ($15/year).

Sierra Club
730 Polk St.
San Francisco, CA 94109–7897
(415) 776–2211

One of the most famous and influential of the environmental organizations. It has 440,000 members, and focuses on wilderness & wildlife preservation, clean air, clean water, and other environmental issues. Makes nature trips available to members. Publishes *Sierra*.

Sinan Company
Natural Building Materials
P.O. Box 857
Davis, CA 95617–0857
(916) 753–3104

Sells paints, lacquers, thinners, and cleaners made from natural products.

Siskiyou Regional Education Project
P.O. Box 220
Cave Junction, OR 97523
(503) 592–4459

Will tell you what you can do to help prevent logging in the proposed new Siskiyou National Park.

Solarex
1335 Piccard Dr.
Rockville, MD 20850–4382
(301) 948–0202

Manufactures photovoltaic equipment.

Southeast Waste Exchange
Urban Institute
University of North Carolina
Charlotte, NC 28223
(704) 547–2307

Source for information on North American waste exchanges, which help businesses find by-products from other businesses that they can then use as raw materials for their own operations.

Spire Corp.
1 Patriots Park
Bedford, MA 01730–2396
(617) 275–6000

Manufactures photovoltaic equipment.

Sunnyside Solar
RD4, Box 808
Brattleboro, VT 05301
(802) 257–1482

Sells solar modules and equipment, high-efficiency appliances and bulbs, etc. Catalog available.

Sunsteam
998 San Antonio Rd.
Palo Alto, CA 94303
(415) 494–9144

Manufactures solar-thermal equipment and supplies solar air conditioning.

Toxicology Information Program
National Institutes of Health
National Library of Medicine
8600 Rockville Pike
Bethesda, MD 20894
(301) 496–6531

Information from the TOXNET computer system about what hazards toxic chemicals pose.

Transitional Network for Appropriate Alternative Technologies (TRANET)
Box 567
Rangely, ME 04970
(207) 864–2252

A clearinghouse for members around the world. Publishes a bimonthly newsletter-directory, *Tranet*.

Transportation Alternatives
494 Broadway
New York, NY 10012
(212) 941–4600

Tree People
12601 Mulholland Dr.
Beverly Hills, CA 90210
(818) 753–4600

Supplies *A Planter's Guide to the Urban Forest* ($10 + $2 shipping & handling).

Trees for Life
1103 Jefferson
Wichita, KS 67203
(316) 263–7294

Sponsors the planting and care of trees in developing countries and has a program to educate children in the U.S. about trees.

Union of Concerned Scientists
26 Church St.
Cambridge, MA 02238
(617) 547-5552

Seeking to stop global warming.

United States Export Council for Renewable Energy
P.O. Box 10095
Arlington, VA 22210-9998
(703) 524-6104

U.S. Public Interest Research Group (PIRG)
215 Pennsylvania Ave., SE
Washington, DC 20036
(202) 546-9707

This is the parent organization of public interest research groups in twenty-one states. It provides information on subjects such as solid waste and toxic materials, and launches legislative battles. Has a million members.

U.S. Windpower
6952 Preston Ave.
Livermore, CA 94550
(415) 455-6012

Manufactures wind energy equipment.

Vanderburgh Enterprises, Inc.
Box 138
Southport, CT 06490
(203) 227-4813

Sells low-flow shower heads, toilet dams, etc.

Water Conservation Systems, Inc.
Damonmill Square, Suite 41-A
Concord, MA 01742
(508) 369-6037; in Massachusetts (800) 462-3341

Sells composting toilets.

Water Pollution Control Federation
601 Wythe St.
Alexandria, VA 22314-1994
(703) 684-2438

Source for a household hazardous waste chart.

Water Resources Research Center
Blaisdell House
University of Massachusetts
Amherst, MA 01003
(413) 545-2842

Wilderness
900 17th St., NW
Washington, DC 20006-2596
(202) 842-3400

Quarterly magazine devoted to preservation of America's forests, deserts, rivers, shores, etc.

Wilderness Society
900 17th St., NW
Washington, DC 20006
(202) 833-2300

Publishes *Wilderness* magazine. Can provide information on the U.S. Forest Service's below-cost timber sales. Educates people on the need to protect public lands and manage them carefully. Has 100,000 members.

Wind Baron
3920 E. Huntington Dr.
Flagstaff, AZ 86004
(602) 526-6400

Manufactures wind-energy equipment.

Windstar Foundation
2317 Snowmass Creek Rd.
Snowmass, CO 81654
(303) 927-4777

Works to inspire and support responsible action. Provides workshops, handbooks, etc. Also sells canvas tote bags. Affiliated with the National Wildlife Federation.

Woods Hole Research Center
P.O. Box 296
Woods Hole, MA 02543
(508) 540-9900

Scientifically investigates (and organizes international meetings on) the greenhouse effect.

Work on Waste (WOW-USA)
82 Judson St.
Canton, NY 13617
(315) 379–9200

Publishes weekly solid waste newsletter for grassroots activists.

Working Group on Community Right-to-Know
215 Pennsylvania Ave., SE
Washington, DC 20003
(202) 546–9707

Supplies information to activists working against toxic substances.

World Neighbors
5116 N. Portland Ave.
Oklahoma City, OK 73112–2098
(405) 946–3333

Encourages self-sufficiency in rural areas of Latin America, Asia, and Africa (places where rain forests are located). Provides training materials in several languages.

World Resources Institute
1709 New York Ave., NW, 17th Floor
Washington, DC 20006
(202) 638–6300

Publishes *World Resources* (an annual assessment of the planet's natural resources) and sponsors programs on pollution, conservation, biological diversity, etc.

World Wildlife Fund
1250 24th St., NW, Suite 500
Washington, DC 20037–1175
(202) 293–4800

Will tell you what you can do about endangered species. Sponsors a program that allows you to help protect an acre of rain forest with a donation of $25. Has 6 million members around the world.

Worldwatch Institute
1776 Massachusetts Ave., NW
Washington, DC 20036
(202) 452–1999

Ask for Worldwatch paper no. 83: *Reforesting the Earth* ($4) and other helpful papers. This is a nonprofit think tank whose *State of the World* report, released each year, is influential. It also publishes the bimonthly magazine *World Watch*.

Appendix B

Directory of Governors, U.S. Senators, and U.S. Representatives

Below is a list of the names and addresses of the Governors of each of the fifty states, and the names of the members of Congress who represent those states. Each member of Congress has at least one specific address, and many have two or more, but mail may be sent by simply addressing it to:

The Honorable [full name of *senator*]
United States Senate
Washington, DC 20510

or:

The Honorable [full name of *representative*]
House of Representatives
Washington, DC 20515

The correct salutations are:

Dear Governor [governor's last name]:

Dear Senator [senator's last name]:
Dear Congressman [representative's last name]:
Dear Congresswoman [representative's last name]:

If you are unable to determine the gender of a representative, use the salutation:

Dear Representative [representative's last name]:

While not as correct, this form will suffice.

All listings are alphabetical by state. Officials elected in the November 5, 1991 election are included, but incumbents, governors-elect, etc., who may have died or left office since that election may not have been deleted. The numbers preceding representatives' names are the numbers of the districts they represent. Nicknames in parentheses are listed for identification only; they should not be used in correspondence.

ALABAMA

Guy Hunt, Governor
Office of the Governor
11 S. Union Street, 2nd Floor
Montgomery, AL 36130

U.S. SENATORS: Howell Heflin
Richard C. Shelby

U.S. REPRESENTATIVES: 1. Sonny Callahan   5. Bud Cramer
2. William L. Dickinson   6. Ben Erdreich
3. Glen Browder   7. Claude Harris
4. Tom Bevill

ALASKA

Walter J. Hickel, Governor
State Capitol
P.O. Box A
Juneau, AK 99811

U.S. SENATORS: Ted Stevens
Frank H. Murkowski

U.S. REPRESENTATIVE: 1. Don Young

ARIZONA

J. Fife Symington III, Governor
State Capitol
1700 W. Washington
Phoenix, AZ 85007

U.S. SENATORS: Dennis DeConcini
John McCain

U.S. REPRESENTATIVES:

1. John J. Rhodes III   4. John L. Kyl
2. Ed Pastor   5. Jim Kolbe
3. Bob Stump

ARKANSAS

Bill Clinton, Governor
250 State Capitol
Office of the Governor
Little Rock, AR 72201

U.S. SENATORS: Dale Bumpers
David H. Pryor

U.S. REPRESENTATIVES:

1. Bill Alexander   3. John Paul Hammerschmidt
2. Ray Thornton   4. Beryl Anthony, Jr.

CALIFORNIA

Pete Wilson, Governor
Governor's Office
P.O. Box 942868
Sacramento, CA 942868–0001

U.S. SENATORS: Alan Cranston
John Seymour

U.S. REPRESENTATIVES:
1. Frank Riggs
2. Wally Herger
3. Robert T. Matsui
4. Vic Fazio
5. Nancy Pelosi
6. Barbara Boxer
7. George Miller
8. Ronald V. Dellums
9. Fortney Pete Stark
10. Don Edwards
11. Tom Lantos
12. Tom Campbell
13. Norman Y. Mineta
14. John T. Doolittle
15. Gary Condit
16. Leon E. Panetta
17. Calvin Dooley
18. Richard H. Lehman
19. Robert J. Lagomarsino
20. William M. Thomas
21. Elton Gallegly
22. Carlos J. Moorhead
23. Anthony C. Beilenson
24. Henry A. Waxman
25. Edward R. Roybal
26. Howard L. Berman
27. Mel Levine
28. Julian C. Dixon
29. Maxine Waters
30. Matthew G. Martinez
31. Mervyn M. Dymally
32. Glenn M. Anderson
33. David Dreier
34. Esteban Edward Torres
35. Jerry Lewis
36. George E. Brown, Jr.
37. Alfred A. (Al) McCandless
38. Robert K. Dornan
39. William E. Dannemeyer
40. C. Christopher Cox
41. Bill Lowery
42. Dana Rohrabacher
43. Ron Packard
44. Randy (Duke) Cunningham
45. Duncan Hunter

COLORADO

Roy Romer, Governor
136 State Capitol Building
Denver, CO 80203

U.S. SENATORS: Timothy E. Wirth
Hank Brown

U.S. REPRESENTATIVES:
1. Patricia Schroeder
2. David E. Skaggs
3. Ben Nighthorse Campbell
4. Wayne Allard
5. Joel Hefley
6. Dan Schaefer

CONNECTICUT

Lowell P. Weicker, Jr., Governor
State Capitol
Hartford, CT 06106

U.S. SENATORS: Christopher J. Dodd
Joseph I. Lieberman

U.S. REPRESENTATIVES: 1. Barbara B. Kennelly
2. Sam Gejdenson
3. Rosa L. DeLauro
4. Christopher Shays
5. Gary A. Franks
6. Nancy L. Johnson

DELAWARE

Michael N. Castle, Governor
Legislative Hall
Dover, DE 19901

U.S. SENATORS: William V. Roth, Jr.
Joseph R. Biden

U.S. REPRESENTATIVE: Thomas A. Carper

FLORIDA

Lawton Chiles, Governor
The Capitol
Tallahassee, FL 32399–0001

U.S. SENATORS: Bob Graham
Connie Mack

U.S. REPRESENTATIVES:
1. Earl Hutto
2. Pete Peterson
3. Charles E. Bennett
4. Craig T. James
5. Bill McCollum
6. Cliff Stearns
7. Sam Gibbons
8. C. W. (Bill) Young
9. Michael Bilirakis
10. Andy Ireland
11. Jim Bacchus
12. Tom Lewis
13. Porter J. Goss
14. Harry Johnston
15. E. Clay Shaw, Jr.
16. Lawrence J. Smith
17. William Lehman
18. Ilena Ros-Lehtinen
19. Dante B. Fascell

GEORGIA

Zell Miller, Governor
203 State Capitol
Atlanta, GA 30334

U.S. SENATORS: Sam Nunn
Wyche Fowler, Jr.

U.S. REPRESENTATIVES:
1. Lindsay Thomas
2. Charles Hatcher
3. Richard Ray
4. Ben Jones
5. John Lewis
6. Newt Gingrich
7. George (Buddy) Darden
8. J. Roy Rowland
9. Ed Jenkins
10. Doug Barnard, Jr.

HAWAII

John D. Waihee III, Governor
State Capitol, 5th Floor
Honolulu, HI 96813

U.S. SENATORS: Daniel K. Inouye
Daniel K. Akaka

U.S. REPRESENTATIVES:
1. Neil Abercrombie
2. Patsy T. Mink

IDAHO

Cecil D. Andrus, Governor
Office of the Governor
State Capitol, 2nd Floor
Boise, ID 83720

U.S. SENATORS: Steve Symms
Larry E. Craig

U.S. REPRESENTATIVES:
1. Larry LaRocco
2. Richard H. Stallings

ILLINOIS

Jim Edgar, Governor
State Capitol
Springfield, IL 62706

U.S. SENATORS: Alan J. Dixon
Paul Simon

U.S. REPRESENTATIVES:
1. Charles A. Hayes
2. Gus Savage
3. Marty Russo
4. George E. Sangmeister
5. William O. Lipinski
6. Henry J. Hyde
7. Cardiss Collins
8. Dan Rostenkowski
9. Sidney R. Yates
10. John Edward Porter
11. Frank Annunzio
12. Philip M. Crane
13. Harris W. Fawell
14. J. Dennis Hastert
15. Thomas W. Ewing
16. John W. Cox, Jr.
17. Lane Evans
18. Robert H. Michel
19. Terry L. Bruce
20. Richard J. Durbin
21. Jerry F. Costello
22. Glenn Poshard

INDIANA

B. Evan Bayh III, Governor
206 State House
Indianapolis, IN 46204

U.S. SENATORS: Richard G. Lugar
Dan Coats

U.S. REPRESENTATIVES:
1. Peter J. Visclosky
2. Philip R. Sharp
3. Timothy J. Roemer
4. Jill L. Long
5. Jim Jontz
6. Dan Burton
7. John T. Myers
8. Frank McCloskey
9. Lee H. Hamilton
10. Andrew Jacobs, Jr.

IOWA

Terry E. Branstad, Governor
Executive Office
Iowa State Capitol
Des Moines, IA 50319

U.S. SENATORS: Chuck Grassley
Tom Harkin

U.S. REPRESENTATIVES:
1. Jim Leach
2. Jim Nussle
3. David R. Nagle
4. Neal Smith
5. Jim Lightfoot
6. Fred Grandy

KANSAS

Joan Finney, Governor
2nd Floor, State Capitol
Topeka, KS 66612

U.S. SENATORS: Bob Dole
Nancy Landon Kassebaum
U.S. REPRESENTATIVES:
1. Pat Roberts
2. Jim Slattery
3. Jan Meyers
4. Dan Glickman
5. Dick Nichols

KENTUCKY

Brereton Jones, Governor
State Capitol, Room 100
Frankfort, KY 40601

U.S. SENATORS: Wendell H. Ford
Mitch McConnell

U.S. REPRESENTATIVES:
1. Carroll Hubbard, Jr.
2. William H. Natcher
3. Romano L. Mazzoli
4. Jim Bunning
5. Harold Rogers
6. Larry J. Hopkins
7. Carl C. Perkins

LOUISIANA

Charles E. (Buddy) Roemer III, Governor
P.O. Box 94004
Baton Rouge, LA 70804–9004

U.S. SENATORS: J. Bennett Johnston
John B. Breaux

U.S. REPRESENTATIVES: 1. Bob Livingston
2. William J. Jefferson
3. W. J. (Billy) Tauzin
4. Jim McCrery
5. Jerry Huckaby
6. Richard H. Baker
7. James A. Hayes
8. Clyde C. Holloway

MAINE

John R. McKernan, Governor
Office of the Governor
State House Station #1
Augusta, ME 04333

U.S. SENATORS: William S. Cohen
George J. Mitchell

U.S. REPRESENTATIVES: 1. Thomas H. Andrews
2. Olympia J. Snowe

MARYLAND

William Donald Schaefer, Governor
State House
Annapolis, MD 21401

U.S. SENATORS: Paul S. Sarbanes
Barbara A. Mikulski

U.S. REPRESENTATIVES: 1. Wayne T. Gilchrest
2. Helen Delich Bently
3. Benjamin L. Cardin
4. C. Thomas McMillen
5. Steny H. Hoyer
6. Beverly B. Bryon
7. Kweisi Mfume
8. Constance A. Morella

MASSACHUSETTS

William F. Weld, Governor
Room 360, State House Executive Office
Boston, MA 02133

U.S. SENATORS: Edward M. Kennedy
John F. Kerry

U.S. REPRESENTATIVES: 1. John W. Olver
2. Richard E. Neal
3. Joseph D. Early
4. Barney Frank
5. Chester G. Atkins
6. Nicholas Mavroules
7. Edward J. Markey
8. Joseph P. Kennedy II
9. John Joseph Moakley
10. Gerry E. Studds
11. Brian J. Donnelly

MICHIGAN

John Engler, Governor
P.O. Box 30026
State Capitol Building
Lansing, MI 48909

U.S. SENATORS: Donald W. Riegle
Carl Levin

U.S. REPRESENTATIVES:
1. Jon Conyers, Jr.
2. Carl D. Pursell
3. Howard Wolpe
4. Frederick S. Upton
5. Paul B. Henry
6. Bob Carr
7. Dale E. Kildee
8. Bob Traxler
9. Guy Vander Jagt
10. Dave Camp
11. Robert W. Davis
12. David E. Bonior
13. Barbara-Rose Collins
14. Dennis M. Hertel
15. William D. Ford
16. John D. Dingell
17. Sander M. Levin
18. William S. Broomfield

MINNESOTA

Arne Carlson, Governor
130 State Capitol
Aurora Avenue
St. Paul, MN 55155

U.S. SENATORS: Dave Durenberger
Paul David Wellstone

U.S. REPRESENTATIVES:
1. Timothy J. Penny
2. Vin Weber
3. Jim Ramstad
4. Bruce F. Vento
5. Martin Olav Sabo
6. Gerry Sikorski
7. Collin C. Peterson
8. James L. Oberstar

MISSISSIPPI

Kirk Fordice, Governor
P.O. Box 139
Jackson, MS 39205

U.S. SENATORS: Thad Cochran
Trent Lott

U.S. REPRESENTATIVES:
1. Jamie L. Whitten
2. Mike Espy
3. G. V. (Sonny) Montgomery
4. Mike Parker
5. Gene Taylor

MISSOURI

John Ashcroft, Governor
Room 216, State Capitol
P.O. Box 720
Jefferson City, MO 65102

U.S. SENATORS: John C. Danforth
Christopher S. Bond

U.S. REPRESENTATIVES: 1. William (Bill) Clay
2. Joan Kelly Horn
3. Richard A. Gephardt
4. Ike Skelton
5. Alan Wheat
6. E. Thomas Coleman
7. Mel Hancock
8. Bill Emerson
9. Harold L. Volkmer

MONTANA

Stan Stephens, Governor
Room 204, Capitol Station
Helena, MT 59620

U.S. SENATORS: Max Baucus
Conrad R. Burns

U.S. REPRESENTATIVES: 1. Pat Williams
2. Ron Marlenee

NEBRASKA

Ben Nelson, Governor
2nd Floor, State Capitol
P.O. Box 94848
Lincoln, NE 68509–4848

U.S. SENATORS: J. James Exon
J. Robert Kerrey

U.S. REPRESENTATIVES: 1. Doug Bereuter
2. Peter Hoagland
3. Bill Barrett

NEVADA

Robert Miller, Governor
Executive Chambers
Capitol Complex
Carson City, NV 89710

U.S. SENATORS: Harry Reid
Richard H. Bryan

U.S. REPRESENTATIVES: 1. James H. Bilbray
2. Barbara F. Vucanovich

NEW HAMPSHIRE

Judd Gregg, Governor
State Capitol
Concord, NH 03301

    U.S. SENATORS: Warren B. Rudman
                   Robert C. Smith

    U.S. REPRESENTATIVES: 1. Bill Zeliff
                           2. Dick Swett

NEW JERSEY

Jim Florio, Governor
State House
Trenton, NJ 08625

    U.S. SENATORS: Bill Bradley
                 Frank R. Lautenberg

    U.S. REPRESENTATIVES:

1. Robert E. Andrews	8. Robert A. Roe
2. William J. Hughes	9. Robert G. Torricella
3. Frank Pallone, Jr.	10. Donald M. Payne
4. Christopher H. Smith	11. Dean A. Gallo
5. Marge Roukema	12. Dick Zimmer
6. Bernard J. Dwyer	13. Jim Saxton
7. Matthew J. Rinaldo	14. Frank J. Guarini

NEW MEXICO

Bruce King, Governor
418 State Capitol
Santa Fe, NM 87503

    U.S. SENATORS: Pete V. Domenici
                 Jeff Bingaman

    U.S. REPRESENTATIVES: 1. Steven Schiff
                           2. Joe Skeen
                           3. Bill Richardson

NEW YORK

Mario M. Cuomo, Governor
Executive Chamber
State Capitol
Albany, NY 12224

U.S. SENATORS: Daniel Patrick Moynihan
Alfonse D'Amato

U.S. REPRESENTATIVES:
1. George J. Hochbrueckner
2. Thomas J. Downey
3. Robert J. Mrazek
4. Norman F. Lent
5. Raymond J. McGrath
6. Floyd H. Flake
7. Gary L. Ackerman
8. James H. Scheuer
9. Thomas J. Manton
10. Charles E. Schumer
11. Edolphus Towns
12. Major R. Owens
13. Stephen J. Solarz
14. Susan Molinari
15. Bill Green
16. Charles B. Rangel
17. Ted Weiss
18. José E. Serrano
19. Eliot L. Engel
20. Nita M. Lowey
21. Hamilton Fish, Jr.
22. Benjamin A. Gilman
23. Michael R. McNulty
24. Gerald B. H. Solomon
25. Sherwood L. Boehlert
26. David O'B. Martin
27. James T. Walsh
28. Matthew F. McHugh
29. Frank Horton
30. Louise McIntosh Slaughter
31. Bill Paxon
32. John J. LaFalce
33. Henry J. Nowak
34. Amo Houghton

NORTH CAROLINA

James G. Martin, Governor
State Capitol
Raleigh, NC 27601–2905

U.S. SENATORS: Jesse Helms
Terry Sanford

U.S. REPRESENTATIVES:
1. Walter B. Jones
2. Tim Valentine
3. H. Martin Lancaster
4. David E. Price
5. Stephen L. Neal
6. Howard Coble
7. Charles Rose
8. W. G. (Bill) Hefner
9. J. Alex McMillan
10. Cass Ballenger
11. Charles H. Taylor

NORTH DAKOTA

George A. Sinner, Governor
1st Floor, State Capitol Building
Bismarck, ND 58505

U.S. SENATORS: Quentin N. Burdick
Kent Conrad

U.S. REPRESENTATIVE: Byron L. Dorgan

OHIO

George V. Voinovich, Governor of Ohio
State House
Columbus, OH 43215

U.S. SENATORS: John Glenn
Howard M. Metzenbaum

U.S. REPRESENTATIVES:
1. Charles Luken
2. Willis D. Gradison, Jr.
3. Tony P. Hall
4. Michael G. Oxley
5. Paul E. Gillmor
6. Bob McEwen
7. David L. Hobson
8. John A. Boehner
9. Marcy Kaptur
10. Clarence E. Miller
11. Dennis E. Eckart
12. John R. Kasich
13. Donald J. Pease
14. Thomas C. Sawyer
15. Chalmers P. Wylie
16. Ralph Regula
17. James A. Traficant, Jr.
18. Douglas Applegate
19. Edward F. Feighan
20. Mary Rose Oakar
21. Louis Stokes

OKLAHOMA

David Walters, Governor
212 State Capitol
Oklahoma City, OK 73105

U.S. SENATORS: David L. Boren
Don Nickles

U.S. REPRESENTATIVES:
1. James M. Inhofe
2. Mike Synar
3. Bill Brewster
4. Dave McCurdy
5. Mickey Edwards
6. Glenn English

OREGON

Barbara Roberts, Governor
254 State Capitol Building
Salem, OR 97310

U.S. SENATORS: Mark O. Hatfield
Bob Packwood

U.S. REPRESENTATIVES:
1. Les AuCoin
2. Robert F. (Bob) Smith
3. Ron Wyden
4. Peter A. DeFazio
5. Michael J. Kopetski

PENNSYLVANIA

Robert P. Casey, Governor
225 Main Capitol Building
Harrisburg, PA 17120

U.S. SENATORS: Arlen Specter
Harris Wofford

U.S. REPRESENTATIVES:
1. Thomas M. Foglietta
2. Lucien Blackwell
3. Robert A. Borski
4. Joe Kolter
5. Richard T. Schulze
6. Gus Yatron
7. Curt Weldon
8. Peter H. Kostmayer
9. Bud Shuster
10. Joseph M. McDade
11. Paul E. Kanjorski
12. John P. Murtha
13. Lawrence Coughlin
14. William J. Coyne
15. Don Ritter
16. Robert S. Walker
17. George W. Gekas
18. Rick Santorum
19. William F. Goodling
20. Joseph M. Gaydos
21. Thomas J. Ridge
22. Austin J. Murphy
23. William F. Clinger, Jr.

RHODE ISLAND

Bruce Sundlun, Governor
222 State House
Providence, RI 02903

U.S. SENATORS: Claiborne Pell
John H. Chafee

U.S. REPRESENTATIVES:
1. Ronald K. Machtley
2. John F. Reed

SOUTH CAROLINA

Carroll A. Campbell, Jr., Governor
State House
P.O. Box 11369
Columbia, SC 29211

U.S. SENATORS: Strom Thurmond
Ernest F. Hollings

U.S. REPRESENTATIVES:
1. Arthur Ravenel, Jr.
2. Floyd Spence
3. Butler Derrick
4. Elizabeth J. Patterson
5. John M. Spratt, Jr.
6. Robin Tallon

SOUTH DAKOTA

George S. Mickelson, Governor
500 East Capitol
Pierre, SD 57501

U.S. SENATORS: Larry Pressler
Thomas A. Daschle

U.S. REPRESENTATIVE: Tim Johnson

TENNESSEE

Ned Ray McWherter, Governor
State Capitol Building
Nashville, TN 37219

U.S. SENATORS: Jim Sasser
Albert Gore, Jr.

U.S. REPRESENTATIVES: 1. James H. (Jimmy) Quillen
2. John J. Duncan, Jr.
3. Marilyn Lloyd
4. Jim Cooper
5. Bob Clement
6. Bart Gordon
7. Don Sundquist
8. John S. Tanner
9. Harold E. Ford

TEXAS

Ann Richards, Governor
Box 12428, Capitol Station
Austin, TX 78711

U.S. SENATORS: Lloyd Bentsen
Phil Gramm

U.S. REPRESENTATIVES: 1. Jim Chapman
2. Charles Wilson
3. Sam Johnson
4. Ralph M. Hall
5. John Bryant
6. Joe Barton
7. Bill Archer
8. Jack Fields
9. Jack Brooks
10. J. J. Pickle
11. Chet Edwards
12. Pete Geren
13. Bill Sarpalius
14. Greg Laughlin
15. E. de la Garza
16. Ronald D. Coleman
17. Charles W. Stenholm
18. Craig A. Washington
19. Larry Combest
20. Henry B. Gonzalez
21. Lamar S. Smith
22. Tom DeLay
23. Albert G. Bustamante
24. Martin Frost
25. Michael A. Andrews
26. Richard K. Armey
27. Solomon P. Ortiz

UTAH

Norman H. Bangerter, Governor
210 State Capitol
Salt Lake City, UT 84114

    U.S. SENATORS: Jake Gern
                    Orrin G. Hatch

    U.S. REPRESENTATIVES: 1. James V. Hansen
                             2. Wayne Owens
                             3. Bill Orton

VERMONT

Richard A. Snelling, Governor
Executive Office
109 State Street
Montpelier, VT 05602

    U.S. SENATORS: Patrick J. Leahy
                    James M. Jeffords

    U.S. REPRESENTATIVE: Bernie Sanders

VIRGINIA

Douglas Wilder, Governor
3rd Floor, Capitol Building
Ricmond, VA 23219

    U.S. SENATORS: John Warner
                    Charles S. Robb

    U.S. REPRESENTATIVES: 1. Herbert H. Bateman   6. Jim Olin
                           2. Owen B. Pickett   7. George Allen
                           3. Thomas J. Bliley, Jr.   8. James P. Moran, Jr.
                           4. Norman Sisisky   9. Rick Boucher
                           5. Lewis F. Payne, Jr.   10. Frank R. Wolf

WASHINGTON

Booth Gardner, Governor
Legislative Building M/S: AS–13
Olympia, WA 98504

    U.S. SENATORS: Brock Adams
                    Slade Gorton

    U.S. REPRESENTATIVES: 1. John Miller   5. Thomas S. Foley
                           2. Al Swift   6. Norman D. Dicks
                           3. Jolene Unsoeld   7. Jim McDermott
                           4. Sid Morrison   8. Rod Chandler

WEST VIRGINIA

Gaston Caperton, Governor
Capitol Building
Charleston, WV 25305

    U.S. SENATORS: Robert C. Byrd
                    John D. Rockefeller IV

    U.S. REPRESENTATIVES: 1. Alan B. Mollohan
                           2. Harley O. Staggers, Jr.
                           3. Robert E. Wise, Jr.
                           4. Nick Joe Rahall II

WISCONSIN

Tommy G. Thompson, Governor
115 East State Capitol
PO Box 7863
Madison, WI 53702

    U.S. SENATORS: Robert Kasten, Jr.
                    Herbert Kohl

    U.S. REPRESENTATIVES: 1. Les Aspin   6. Thomas E. Petri
                           2. Scott L. Klug   7. David R. Obey
                           3. Steve Gunderson   8. Toby Roth
                           4. Gerald D. Kleczka 9. F. James Sensenbrenner, Jr.
                           5. Jim Moody

WYOMING

Michael J. Sullivan, Governor
State Capitol
Cheyenne, WY 82002

    U.S. SENATORS: Malcolm Wallop
                  Alan Simpson

    U.S. REPRESENTATIVE: Craig Thomas